One He

One Heart, One Voice

The rich and varied resource of music in worship

Andrew Maries

HODDER AND STOUGHTON
LONDON   SYDNEY   AUCKLAND   TORONTO

To David and Anne Watson without whose vision and encouragement this book would not have been written.

Illustrations by Janet Lunt

The front cover is designed from a banner made at St. Michael-le-Belfrey

British Library Cataloguing in Publication Data

Maries, Andrew
   One heart, one voice.
   1. Music in churches   2. Church music——
   History and criticism
   I. Title
   264'.2   BV290
   ISBN 0 340 38343 7

CONTENTS

'May the God of steadfastness and encouragement grant you to live in such harmony with one another, in accord with Christ Jesus, that together you may with one voice glorify the God and Father of our Lord Jesus Christ' Rom. 15:5–6.

PREFACE

'It's one of those books that once you put it down,
you simply can't pick it up!'

So wrote one critic on one of the thousands of wordy
tomes published each year. I suppose every author
hopes that his book will be different, so before you lay
this one aside for good, let me tell what it is about.

As the title implies, *One Heart, One Voice* is about the
harmony of music and relationships, two areas at the
very heart of worship. Many aspects of church life have
undergone radical change over the last few decades.
Nowhere is this more true than in the area of music in
worship. Yet there have been few guidelines available for
churches and musicians trying to come to terms with this
changing scene. Many times in our own development, at
St. Michael's, we could have benefited from a book
which gave some help in seeking a balanced path in the
renewal of church music today.

Ultimately, I decided to try and do something about it
myself! My purpose: to give vision and encouragement
for the creative use of music in worship and to show that
there can and should be a balanced integration of old and
new. My perspective: the local congregation of mixed
ability and resources. My authority: many years of experience with my fellow members in a congregation
which has been working out the renewal of its life and
worship in the setting of an historic denomination.

The story of renewal in St. Michael's, and its earlier
sister church St. Cuthbert's, is well known and is told in
David Watson's autobiography *You Are My God*. Because

of the eclectic nature of the congregation, and a pooling
and channelling of resources, it has been possible for us
to open up and develop many new aspects of church life,
particularly in worship and the arts. While this has been
exceptional and unique to St. Michael's in some respects,
it would be easy to dismiss our experience as having no
relevance to the local scene. We have been fortunate in
having one or two 'experts' like myself, who have been
able to provide continuity and draw out others' gifts, but
the building blocks of our life as a church, and particularly in its music, have been humble ordinary lives. All
that we have achieved has hinged on people's availability: availability to the Holy Spirit to be personally renewed; availability to the Body of Christ to be built
together in love and commitment; availability to the
leadership to be equipped and trained for ministry.

This is especially important and is why I believe the
things I have to share in this book are of universal
application whether we are worshipping in a small country church, a city church like our own, or even a
cathedral. The book seeks to draw out foundational
principles for the use of music in worship and is
earthed in practical experience. To come to terms with it
at all may, for some, require a radical rethink of their
present approach.

My own involvement stems from almost the earliest
days. It was one foggy, February evening in 1968 when I
first came to York. I had come for an interview to study
music at the university and imagined York as one of those
big, black cities of the north of England. How surprised I
was next morning when I woke to brilliant sunshine and
to one of the most beautiful medieval cities in Europe!

It was almost by chance that I came at all. The university was bottom on my list of six but I happened to play a
piece by the interviewer's favourite composer and the

department was desperately in need of an oboist for the university orchestra! I started that same autumn.

My first visit to St. Cuthbert's was similarly 'by chance'. My room-mate had been invited to play his violin in a special 'guest' service and, with nothing better to do, I offered him a lift. I knew nothing of the church I was going to but was tremendously impressed by the clear and authoritative preaching of the minister, David Watson, and the enormous warmth and enthusiasm of the packed congregation. My friend couldn't wait to get out, but for me a relationship with the church began which has changed the pattern and direction of my life and which continues down to the present day.

After university I worked for a year in London, never expecting to come back to York, but to my surprise I returned to play the organ at St. Cuthbert's in the autumn of 1972. Almost immediately, early in 1973, the congregation moved en masse into the near-redundant church of St. Michael-le-Belfrey, next to the Minster and right in the heart of historic York. In that year I became a member of the rectory household and was eventually totally supported in the evolving task of Director of Music. No one has been more surprised than I at how things have developed, and I have been thrilled to see how God has used my gifts in ways I could never have imagined.

I owe the development of this ministry to the vision of David and Anne Watson who soon saw the vital role worship played in the life of the Church. They were willing to give themselves sacrificially to see this vision fulfilled and made it possible practically for me to devote myself to nurturing our worship life through the gift of music.

There have been many battles and traumas along the way but one source of enormous encouragement and inspiration has come consistently from members of the

Church of the Holy Redeemer, Houston, Texas and their travelling team, the Fisherfolk. Their personal wholeness and integrity gave us all a vision of life together in the Body of Christ and a musical expression which could be both sensitive and varied, contemporary and classical. They gave me hope that the music of renewal could combine warmth and spontaneity with musical worth.

I must also acknowledge a debt to many others within our own fellowship who have, over the years, given themselves to our music and to our worship life in the fulfilment of this vision. They have a very special and significant part in the pages of this book.

More specifically, I must express my appreciation for all the practical help I have received from many people in putting this book together. My wife Alicia and the office staff have shown amazing patience and restraint in the interminable process of writing it. There will be great rejoicing in our offices when they finally see it in print! I have already had two celebrations on finishing it – only to find that I hadn't! The third is yet to come!

Thank you Pippa, Nigel, Judy, Jeni, Tina and Anne for your help with the typing and our Parochial Church Council for allowing me the time to write. Thank you too, Paul Burbridge, for reading the manuscript and for the many helpful comments on structure and literary style which will help many readers make it to the end! Also, my thanks to Geoff and Cazz Colmer for wading through the first draft and whose helpful comments enabled the book to widen its perspective. Finally thank you Carolyn Armitage, my patient editor, for the opportunity to share our experience with many thousands of others for whom I hope *One Heart, One Voice* will become a useful hand-book on the subject of music in worship.

Andrew Maries July 1985

FOREWORD

Talk to any octogenarian and you will discover a person who has seen more change in a lifetime than anyone living prior to the twentieth century. Talk to any minister or church musician and you will discover a person who is – willingly or not – coming to grips with enormous change within an institution subject to history yet dedicated to an unchanging God.

In this eminently approachable and helpful book, Andrew Maries looks at the recent renewal movement in the Christian Church as an instrument of change and asks, "What was the significance of it all, and what have we learned?"

Focusing his attention on worship as the corporate heartbeat of Christianity, he invites the reader to share many of the experiences and insights of what happened at St. Michael-le-Belfrey in York under the visionary leadership of the late David Watson. Clearly this happening was – and is – one into which the author has poured his life's energy. Drawing upon this experience and upon biblical and ecclesiastical sources, he weaves a tapestry of thought which is illuminating and challenging for today's worship leader. At the same time, the chapters are replete with practical help for the ordinary, garden-variety church with no illusions of grandeur! Above all, there is warmth and tenderness here which reveal a heart of love for God's gathered people, the Church.

Betty Pulkingham

1

LOOKING BACK

'History repeats itself – it has to, no one ever listens!'

Many people are very ignorant of the Bible and Early Church music. Many of the new things we are experiencing find echoes in the experience of past generations: renewal is a re-discovery of those roots. Looking back at our history can bring us to a clearer and more authentic use of music in worship and give some firm and foundational principles which we may apply to our experience today.

ONE. MUSIC IN THE BIBLE

Old Testament

1) Use of Music

All through the Bible the composing and performing of music was central to the worship and daily life of God's people. It was woven into the fabric of their lives. Music was used to celebrate national events such as the successful Exodus from Egypt (Exod. 15) or the entry of the Ark to Jerusalem (1 Chr. 15–16). It was used in battle to summon the troops or signal the collapse of the walls of Jericho (Josh. 6:20), even as a weapon against the enemy

(2 Chr. 20:21). Music was used extensively in religious ceremony and the regular liturgy of worship in the Temple, for which the book of Psalms was created as a musical psalter. Music was used to emphasise important events and particularly to heighten the significance of religious activities.

But music also had an 'ordinary' face. It was a natural expression of personal and corporate emotion. People sang for great joy and thanksgiving such as Hannah (1 Sam. 2) and Mary (Luke 1:46–55); or out of their deep grief as David's lament for the death of Jonathan (2 Sam. 1). Music was used at sacred and secular feasts (Isa. 5:12), social events (mentioned at the return of the prodigal son in Luke 15:25), in work songs as people harvested the crops (Isa. 16:10), and in the expression of love (Song of Songs).

Reading about the ways people in the Bible used their music can enrich our own understanding of the place of music in worship, either in its social function of uniting the people in their praise and worship of God or in helping them to express their unique identity as a chosen race. We can see it used as a spiritual weapon and as a vehicle for ministry. Whatever its function, it increased people's awareness of the God who was among them; an experience which was constantly changing and developing and evoking a fresh response in each generation.

2) Type of Music

Whatever we know about music in the Bible, we know little of how it really sounded! It was never written down and we may only guess at its characteristics from descriptions of the types of instruments used and from archaeological relics which have survived. One thing is clear – it would have been very different indeed from our own music. For example, Western music has a well-defined sense of rhythm and harmony and the music progresses in a continuous line from beginning to end. It has a clear beat, usually a clearly-defined structure and a sense of climax and achievement.

In contrast, much ancient Jewish music would probably have had less sense of rhythm, although for dance some kind of rhythmic music must have existed. This may have resembled the ancient folk music still to be heard in the Middle East with its nasal singing, quavering flutes and insistent drums. Most singing and playing would have been in unison. I suspect that much of it would shock and mystify our own ears, much as the traditional music of Malaya and Japan seems so strange to us today. Imagine, for instance, the effect of one hundred and twenty trumpet-playing priests sounding forth at the dedication of the Temple in Jerusalem! (2 Chr. 5). Even the worst school band could hardly have competed with such a sound!

Ancient Hebrew instruments were crude and in Psalm 150 one can find a reasonable catalogue of the types in use. These fall into three categories:

Stringed Instruments
  Harp or Lyre (Heb. *Kinnôr*) – small and portable and possibly played with a plectrum (Gen. 4:21 & 1 Sam. 16:23).
  Psaltry or Lute (Heb. *Nēbel*) – plucked with the fingers (1 Sam. 10:5).
  Trigon – a triangular harp of high pitch (Dan. 3:5).

Wind Instruments
  Pipe (Heb. *Hālîl* or *Aulos*) – possibly a reed instrument like the oboe.
  Flute – blown across a hole.
  The pipe or flute was used in festival processions (Isa. 30:29), national celebrations (1 Kgs 1:40) but also for mourning (Matt. 9:23) and on solemn occasions (Jer. 48:36).

Organ (Heb. *Ugàb*) – a generic term covering all wind instruments (Gen. 4:21).

Horn (Heb. *Qeren*) An early trumpet-like instrument made from animal horn (Dan. 3:7).

Trumpet:1. (Heb. *Shofar*) – a long ram's horn used for ceremonial or military occasions. Frequently used in the Old Testament.

2. (Heb. *Hasōserâ*) – a silver instrument used for sacred occasions (Num. 10:1–10).

Percussion Instruments

Bells – worn on ceremonial clothing with no musical function, but used to signify the presence of God e.g. Aaron's robes (Ex. 28:35).

Cymbals – large or small, cupped or flat (Ps. 150).

Timbrel (Heb. *Tōp*) – a festive and joyful instrument held and struck by the hand (Ex. 15:20, Isa. 5:12, 1 Sam. 18:6).

Drums – of varying sizes shown in contemporary reliefs.

A great deal of symbolic significance was invested in these instruments, particularly in the *Shofar* or trumpet, which is still used in Jewish synagogues today. It marks the beginning and end of major festivals. Certain instruments accompanied certain ceremonies. The Psalms give instructions as to which ones were to be used in the accompaniment of the set chant.

Psalm 75 has the instruction: 'To the choirmaster: according to "Do Not Destroy". A Psalm of Asaph. A Song.'

Psalm 76 says: 'To the choirmaster: with stringed instruments.' There are many other examples.

3) Music for Liturgy

Music was so important in the life of Israel that when the nation became more established King David set about organising music and musicians for the main focus of national life – its worship.

1 Chr. 15 and 25 relate in detail the manpower and resources invested to provide the very best for the service of God. There were, for example, two hundred and eighty-eight musicians, all chosen from the priestly tribe of Levi. These were skilful in their duties, whether in singing or playing instruments, and had a close relationship with the other priests who conducted the constant series of religious ceremonies which formed the pattern of daily life in Israel.

When the Ark was settled in its place in Jerusalem, several of the leading musicians heralded its arrival and were positioned at the heart of the procession. They were then appointed as 'ministers' before the Ark 'to invoke, to thank and to praise the Lord day by day'. They, with Heman and Jeduthan, were 'expressly named to give thanks to the Lord' (1 Chr. 16:41).

The music was viewed as a most serious matter worthy of detailed attention and careful preparation. A huge infrastructure was created to serve the religious ceremonies of the Temple and to ensure that there was a constant offering of praise and thanksgiving with music.

Here we see how careful organisation and preparation can go hand in hand with the spontaneous activity of God. For some people today the two are quite irreconcilable. How can the free, spontaneous activity of the Holy Spirit be married with rigid ecclesiastical structures? It is interesting to compare the passages in 1 Chronicles about the ordering of Temple music with 2 Chronicles 5 where we read of the Ark being brought into the newly dedi-

cated Temple amid tremendous festivity and ceremonial.
On this occasion hundreds of priests and musicians were
involved in an historic moment. The Ark, which symbol-
ised the presence of God with His people, was to be given
a permanent resting place within the Temple sanctuary.
Countless sacrifices were made, the Ark was deposited in
the Holy of Holies and, on the reappearance of the
priests, the singers and musicians began to give praise to
the Lord singing, 'For he is good, for his steadfast love
endures for ever.'

At this point something happened – 'The house, the
house of the Lord, was filled with a cloud, so that the
priests could not stand to minister for the glory of the
Lord filled the house of God.' They were well into their
carefully prepared and rehearsed liturgy when God in-
tervened. When they began to praise God with their
music, the reality of God's presence was realised physically within the building. Furthermore, the writer makes
a special point of telling us that they did this in 'unison' or
'with one voice'. Having given themselves to the Lord
and prepared the music, God honoured their sincerity
and oneness of heart by revealing his glory to them. How
gracious of God to honour a man-made order, waiting
until it had reached a convenient moment before con-
firming human activity with a manifestation of his
presence!

For those who believe that all tradition or ceremonial is
inhibiting to the work of the Holy Spirit, notice the huge
scale and seriousness of their preparations. For those
who prefer the familiarity of a more structured form of
worship, take note of the spontaneity and responsiveness to the Spirit which co-existed happily with the
religious ceremonial.

The beauty of this Old Testament example is that
people were able to accept a regular routine expression
for their worship, almost as a discipline, while remaining

open to change and ready to adapt to a God of power and movement.

4) Music for Praise

There are three main words commonly used in the Bible for our English word 'praise'. These are:

Hálal – making a noise
Zámar – singing or playing music
Yàdâ – moving the body

a) Hálal – This first and universal word gives us 'Hallelujah' meaning 'praise Yah(weh).' The Jews only spoke the first syllable of God's name out of reverence. Its noun *tehilláh* is mainly used to express the mighty and transcendent character of God: 'His glory covered the heavens and the earth was full of his *praise*' (Hab. 3:3).

'Then my tongue shall tell of thy righteousness and of thy *praise* all the day long' (Ps. 35:28).

Its basic meaning is 'to make a noise' and is characteristic of the Hebrew practice of expressing praise and prayer and reading the scriptures out loud. The Ethiopian in Acts 8:30 is reading Isaiah 53 loud enough to be heard by Philip as he comes alongside. On the other hand, when Eli finds Hannah praying silently but moving her lips, he thinks she is drunk (1 Sam. 1:12–15).

Often in the Psalms the word for praise is linked to another word: *Rua*, meaning 'make a joyful noise'. So in Psalm 66:1–2 we read:

> '*Make a joyful noise* to God, all the earth;
> Sing the glory of his name;
> Give to him glorious *praise*.'

Of course praising and making a noise, especially a joyful noise, usually implies singing. Consequently many references mention the singing of praise like those above.

However, our praise need not be highly cultured to be acceptable to God. Those of us whose singing verges on the side of 'noise-making' can take heart!

b) Zámar – This word for singing or playing an instrument covers musical activity and could be translated as 'making melody'. When God acted in people's lives their natural response was to sing his praise. There are countless references particularly in the Psalms:

Psalm 18:49   'Therefore I will praise you among the
              nations, O Lord;
              I will sing praises to your name.' (NIV)
Psalm 147:1   'It is good to sing praises to our God;
              For he is gracious and a song of praise is
              seemly.'
and v.7   'Sing to the Lord with thanksgiving;
              Make melody to our God upon the lyre.'

This kind of praise could be sung or played. Individuals could offer it (Ps. 108:1–3) and whole congregations (Ps. 47:6–9). Specialist choirs could sing their praises antiphonally (Ps. 136 or Ps. 118:1–4). Thus all are gathered into musical praise, whatever their level of ability.

c) Yàdâ – Sometimes singing and making a joyful noise wasn't enough to express a person's praise: there must be bodily movement as well. This was such a natural response that our own translations give no indication that bodily gesture is implied in the word 'praise'. Yet the word means 'to stretch out the hand'. Just as kneeling is naturally associated with prayer so for the Hebrew to pray and praise meant lifting hands towards God as a simple gesture of openness and submission (see Ps. 63:3–4 and Ps. 134:2). Frequently the same word is translated as 'giving thanks'. At special times of spiritual activity the worshipper 'praised' or 'gave thanks' with his whole body. The Hebrew word for worship reinforces this idea meaning 'to bow down', as we shall see later. Both are linked in this passage from 2 Chronicles 7:3 (NIV): 'When all the Israelites saw the fire coming down and the glory of the Lord above the temple, they knelt on the pavement with their faces to the ground and they worshipped and gave thanks to the Lord.'

Another example is Psalm 138:1–2 –

'I give thee thanks, O Lord, with my whole heart;
Before the gods I sing thy *praise*;
I bow down towards thy holy temple.'

While we suffer from 'ecclesiastical rigor mortis', the ancient worshipper knew no self-consciousness in his relationship to God. Praise could frequently be extremely exuberant! While people sometimes prostrated themselves on the ground in humble reverence, and lifted hands in prayer, they also clapped their hands, shouted their praises and danced:

Psalm 47:1–
'*Clap* your hands all you people,
Shout to God with *loud songs* of joy!'

Psalm 149:3–
'Let them praise his name with *dancing*,
Making melody to him with timbrel and lyre!
For the Lord takes pleasure in his people;
He adorns the humble with victory.'

God is pleased when his people get excited about him as long as they remain humble and their praise is genuine. Today, we are often embarrassed by such overt emotion. While we should be aware of the dangers of a fleshly emotionalism, we should not be frightened of a

more extrovert expression of our love for God. <u>But
exuberance in praise should not imply shoddiness in
technique or presentation</u>:

Psalm 33:1–3 –
    'Praise befits the upright.
    Praise the Lord with the lyre,
    Make melody to him with the harp of ten strings!
    Sing to him a new song,
    Play skilfully on the strings,
    With loud shouts.'

New Testament

1) Musical References

While the Old Testament has many complete songs*
examples in the New Testament are more difficult to find.
The lack of musical reference in general can be attributed
to the unsettled state of the Early Church and the conditions which prevailed at the time which made any
artistic expression difficult. Nevertheless, in the first two
chapters of Luke, three songs appear:
    The Song of Mary or Magnificat (Luke 1:46–55)
    The Song of Zechariah or Benedictus (Luke 1:68–79)
    The Song of Simeon or Nunc Dimittis (Luke 2:29–32)
    The Song of Mary follows the visitation of the angel to
announce the news that she will bear the holy Son of
God. It bears remarkable resemblances to Hannah's song

---

  * The Songs of Moses Exod. 15 and Deut. 32
    Hannah's Song 1 Samuel 2:2–20
    David's Laments
    The whole of the Psalms
    The Song of Songs
    The Song of Hezekiah Isa. 38:10–11
    The Lamentations of Jeremiah

in the Old Testament. Perhaps Mary was recalling familiar phrases and images from Jewish praise as she gave glory to God a short time later when she visited Elizabeth. As with Hannah, the birth of her son is seen in the wider context of God's greater activity among his people.

The Song of Zechariah echoes this same characteristic Jewishness. It is a benediction or blessing of God for bringing redemption to his people in accordance with ancient prophecies and the covenant made by God. But the text tells us that Zechariah prophesied. The hymn therefore changes mood in verse 76, where it is specifically directed towards the future mission of John who will 'go before the Lord and prepare his ways'. Verse 79 recalls the two passages from Isaiah 9:2 and 59:8.

The Song of Simeon is the third hymn from these early chapters of Luke which, like the others, has been traditionally sung in Christian worship from the beginning. Who knows whether their first renderings were in song? Simeon takes the baby Jesus in his arms and blesses God for the fulfilment of a promise that he would see the coming of the Messiah before he died.

Other references include Luke 2 where a window is opened on the praise and worship of heaven itself. The heavenly choir appears in person to hail the Saviour at his birth (13–14). A musician can always be excited by the thought that, of all earthly activities, music is the one that continues to glorify God for all eternity! Later in the Gospels we read of Jesus and the disciples singing a hymn at the close of the Last Supper (Matt. 26:30 and Mark 14:26). This was probably the second part of the '*Hallel*' given in Psalms 115 to 118, traditionally sung at the end of the Passover meal. In Acts 16:25, Paul and Silas were singing hymns in prison when an earthquake burst open the doors and set them free. What power there is in musical praise!

Despite the lack of specific references, it is clear that the singing of spiritual songs was an integral part of the worship of the Early Church as witnessed by 1 Cor. 14:15–16 and James 5:13, the canticles already mentioned in Luke, and the many doxologies recorded here and there.

Songs were used as a spontaneous expression of joy and praise and also as a means of instruction. The three-fold division of psalms, hymns and spiritual songs can be useful if taken generally.

Psalms: These were based on the Old Testament pattern and would include the three canticles of Luke. Because of the close links with synagogue worship, early Christians would have used the traditional Psalms as we do today.

Hymns: A hymn was expected to have some doctrinal and didactic purpose and so in this category might come the passages in the New Testament characterised by their poetic form and credal content. Such passages shine out from the surrounding narrative and many are thought to contain fragments of early hymns – John 1:1–18, Phil. 2:6–11, Eph. 1:3–14, Eph. 5:14, 2 Tim. 2:11–13, Titus 3:4–7.

Songs: These would include the short doxologies mentioned above: Luke 2:14, 1 Tim. 1:17, 1 Tim. 6:15–16 and several parts of the book of Revelation: 4:8, 11; 5:9, 12, 13; 7:12 etc. Many of these might have been used in corporate worship much as some of the shorter simpler songs are used in informal worship today. Perhaps they had a more spontaneous nature, maybe directly inspired by the Spirit, as indicated in the scene given in 1 Cor. 14:26 – 'Each one has a hymn, a lesson, a revelation.'

This category should also include some reference to *'Singing in the Spirit'* mentioned by St. Paul in 1 Cor. 14:15. This was improvised singing, often corporate and often using the gift of tongues. This phenomenon has been reappearing in the worship of the Church over the last few decades in charismatic renewal. The Pentecostal Churches had their birth in such experiences at the turn of the century. As we shall see later, these spiritual gifts, once thought to have died out with the early Christians, have been exercised almost continually in one part or another of the life of the Church, right up to the present day.

Another passage, Ephesians 5:18–20, links being filled with the Spirit to 'Addressing one another in psalms, hymns and spiritual songs, singing and making melody to the Lord with all your heart.' Surely the latter phrase 'making melody' could have some reference to 'Singing in the Spirit'.

These passages put the use of music in the New Testament firmly in the context of Christian fellowship, as an expression of the worship and love of a united body of believers. This is described in Col. 3:12–17 which could be paraphrased thus:

God's people, loved and chosen by him(12), are those bound together by the perfect unity of love and forgiveness(13–15). A rich and varied worship ensues, which is characterised by the singing of psalms, hymns and spiritual songs with great thankfulness to God.

The music is a vehicle for praise and worship, but also for mutual encouragement, correction and teaching. Often it enshrines the basic tenets of belief and helps people to establish their identity as believers. Through music they are able to become the One Voice of the One Body reflecting in the harmony of the music the harmony of their relationships in Christ: 'May the God of steadfastness and encouragement grant you to live in such harmony with one another, in accord with Christ Jesus, that together you may with one voice glorify the God and Father of our Lord Jesus Christ' (Rom. 15:5–6).

2) Contemporary Jewish Worship

Music was obviously an integral part of the life of the
Early Church, despite turmoil and persecution. While
most of it was initially fairly informal, the early liturgical
music drew on its Jewish roots for sustenance and inspiration. Perhaps we don't realise how much our
Christian worship had its sources within Judaism.

Our forms of service were modelled at first on those
used in the Jewish synagogues. Elements of singing
psalms and songs of praise, reading the scriptures, hearing a sermon, saying prayers, were all carried over into
Christian liturgy.

The *Eucharist* itself was derived partly from synagogue
practices. It had two distinct halves: The first had an
educational function and was open to all, including
unbelievers. Like synagogue worship it included readings from scripture and a sermon. The second half was
specifically for committed Christians, in which the commands of Christ to break bread and drink wine as a sign
of his death and of his coming again were obeyed. Even
this had echoes of Judaism in the celebration of the
Passover and the Last Supper. Initially the first part took
place in the synagogue and the second in people's
homes, but over the first four centuries this was eventually combined into one act of worship.

Music had an important part in all these activities. It set
apart the worship of God from the everyday. During this
period, pure vocal music was considered the most perfect
expression of praise to God, because instrumental music
was thought to be tainted with paganism. Perhaps
people had forgotten an earlier belief represented in
Psalm 150 that every voice and instrument could be
employed worshipfully!

In the synagogue the psalms were sung regularly in a
variety of ways. In *responsorial singing* the leader or 'pre-

centor' was a specially trained Levite who sang the psalm by half verses while the congregation repeated what was sung. Sometimes with certain psalms, called *Hallel* psalms, he would sing through the psalm with the congregation using the first 'Hallelujah' as a *refrain*. Other methods included singing straight through the psalm with everyone participating, if it was simple enough, or singing *antiphonally* in which the two halves of the congregation answered each other with alternate verses.

Readings from scripture were organised in a liturgical year just like some of our own services. They were also intoned to complicated musical formulae developed over the centuries and handed down orally. It is interesting to think of Jesus, in Luke 4:18, *singing* the famous passage from Isaiah according to the custom of the day, and then relating it directly to himself.

As well as psalms and readings, there were also songs of a more intimate nature. Chants used for the psalms emphasised the meaning and structure of the text. But in a song the melody could be more expressive of emotion. There was the *Shema*, a sort of Jewish creed and the *Kedushah* similar to the Sanctus; 'Holy, Holy, Holy.'

The Church received many of those raised in the culture and practice of the synagogue into its number. The existing pattern of worship was thus inherited by the Christians. This period stands as a bridge between the Jewish and Christian traditions showing a continuous and organic development from one to the other. Many of the oldest chants of the Church have been identified with ancient Jewish melodies – just one example of the intimate relationship that existed between the two. There is never in history a complete break between one period and another. Christianity maintained its essential Jewishness for a long time after its birth. We can therefore trace a continuous line from our present musical tradition back, through Church history, to the pages of the Bible.

TWO: MUSIC IN THE CHURCH

Music presented the Early Church with a problem: it could heighten faith, but it could also distract. The prolific writings and homilies of the first few centuries often address themselves to the priority of ensuring that music in worship glorified God and edified the people of God. The music was constantly to yield first place to the words. Singing was to be filled with the Holy Spirit and a conscious expression of the faith. Worldly music was a major seductive force; but for the exhortations to sing in worship found in the Scriptures, some Church Fathers might have been tempted to ban it altogether! However, St. Augustine wrote, 'Apart from those moments when the Scriptures are being read or a sermon is preached, when the bishop is praying aloud or the deacon is specifying the intentions of the litany of community prayer, is there any time when the faithful assembled in the church are not singing? Truly I see nothing better, more useful or more holy that they could do!'

1) Musical Forms

These continued to develop the legacy from the Hebrew world. St. Ambrose praised the value of *psalm singing*: 'They too sing their psalms well, as psalms are sweet for every age and are becoming to each sex . . . they create a great bond of unity when the whole people raise their voices in one choir.' By their association with particular melodies they could be remembered and sung by all people. Among the Syrian monasteries *antiphonal* singing of the Psalms was modelled on the ancient Temple practice of the Old Testament. This was then carried to the rest of the church by St. Ambrose.

Ambrose was also instrumental in developing the form of the *hymn*. The hymn continued in importance as a

means of enshrining doctrine and the centrality of Christ.
Some hymns were modelled on Greek odes, but most
originated around Alexandria in the East, where, like folk
songs, they were accompanied with hand-clapping and
dance movements. Eventually such pagan influences
were frowned upon and the Church authorities clamped
down on these practices, reforming hymn singing and
allowing only Biblical texts and a few others to be used.
Hymns were originally introduced to the Latin Church by
Hilary of Poitiers and then encouraged by Ambrose,
particularly at one time of persecution: 'At this time it was
here first instituted after the manner of the Eastern
Churches, that hymns and psalms should be sung, lest
the people should wax faint through the tediousness of
sorrow: which custom being retained from that day to
this, is still imitated by divers, yea, almost by all Thy
congregations throughout other parts of the world.'

The Ambrosian hymn usually consisted of eight verses
with four lines in each. Their regularity of form made
them very popular and, because they were intended for
congregational participation, they kept their simplicity.
Simple devotional songs also had their place in early Church
worship. St. Paul is surely referring to these when he
talks about spiritual songs in his teaching on the Body of
Christ. (Eph. 5:19). Such songs did not aspire to great
artistic achievement but were simply a vehicle for praise
and adoration. One can imagine the first 'Love Feasts'
being peppered with prayers and such songs as the
believers gathered for a common evening meal.

Another part of liturgical singing was the *Gradual*, so
called because it was sung from the altar steps or 'gradus'
by the deacon. It occurred between the readings in the
Eucharist.

A further aspect of church music at this time was the
practice of singing an 'Alleluia' as a people's refrain to
the singing of the Psalms by the cantor. This stemmed

from the synagogue and in the first centuries it became increasingly common among Eastern Churches. Such singing became highly ornamental, sometimes being improvised for more than a quarter of an hour, as is still the practice in parts of the Egyptian Coptic Church. The 'Alleluia' became an important part of the liturgy and was very popular among congregations as an exclamation of Christian joy.

2) Improvisation

We should realise that *improvised singing* held a most important place in the worship of these early centuries. St. John Chrysostom describes this: 'Though men and women, young and old, are different, when they sing hymns, their voices are influenced by the Holy Spirit in such a way that the melody sounds as if sung by one voice.'

He also refers to the widespread practice of responsorial singing, where the cantor sings a verse and the congregation answers with a refrain. He calls him a prophet: 'The prophet speaks and we all respond to him. All of us make echo to him. Together we form one choir. In this, earth imitates heaven. This is the nobility of the Church.' Perhaps this too was improvised, as St. Cassiodorus implies: 'The tongue of singers rejoices in it; joyfully the community repeats it.'*

The most significant aspect of improvised singing was the practice of *jubilation*. This was a melismatic elaboration of the last syllable of the word 'Alleluia'. An 'Alleluia' was sung before the Gospel and the congregation could be so moved that they improvised on the final 'a' for as long as five minutes, as a preparation for listening to the word of God. The oriental Christian was well

* As quoted in *L'encyclopédie des Musiques Sacres* (Paris: Editions Lagerie. 1968–79) Vol. 2 p. 15.

practiced in this form (like yodelling, people would jubilate naturally, at work in the fields or at sea), but the
Western Christian needed more explanation. There were
therefore many references to jubilation in the writing of
the Church Fathers strongly recommending it.

Pope Gregory: 'What we mean by the term jubilation is
when we conceive such a great joy in the heart that we
cannot express it in words; yet, despite this, the heart
vents what it is feeling by means of the voice what it
cannot express by discursive speech . . . Let angels therefore praise, because they know such brightness; but let
men, who are limited by speech, jubilate.'

St. Augustine describes it as 'singing on vowel sounds'
and there were other parts of the service when it could
occur, such as graduals and offertories. Its similarity
to the modern charismatic experience of singing in
tongues or singing in the Spirit cannot be overlooked. An
article in *L'encyclopédie de la Musique* on improvisation
sums up the descriptions of the Church Fathers:

From these sources one senses clearly that the music of
the Christian era was originally improvised. The first
Christians expressed their religious ecstasy in a purely
emotional and spontaneous fashion by means of
music. According to the terminology of Tertullian, all
the members of an assembly were invited to participate
in the praise of God by words from Scripture or by
'songs of their own invention'. The first Christian
authors, Hilary of Poitiers (315–366) and Jerome
(340–420) and Augustine (354–430) until Amalris
(9th C) describe the rich, exuberant coloraturas sung
without a text, and the Alleluia songs as overwhelming melodies of joy and gratitude sung upon the
inspiration of the moment. A large number of the
melodies that have come down to us still have traces
of improvisation.

3) Establishment

With the third century it became possible for Christians to congregate in public, instead of hiding in the Catacombs, and by the end of the century some Christian churches were as big as some of the pagan temples. The Roman Church abandoned the original Greek liturgy in favour of its own and the Eastern and Western Churches began to develop their traditions separately. Until then the practice had been to develop local liturgies upon a common, accepted foundation. In 313 Constantine legitimised the Church, and music and liturgy were able to grow and establish themselves in more stable circumstances. But heresies necessitated the fixing and unifying of liturgical texts. So Christian worship gradually began to lose some of its spontaneity as it became a general and public religion. This process has continued down to the present day.

4) Styles of Worship

Meanwhile, worship was often very lively and might remind us today more of a Pentecostal meeting. St. Augustine's own congregation in the early fifth century reacted to what was happening in the service with considerable emotion. He describes a member of the congregation during the singing of a psalm: 'You will see him singing with intense emotion, with the expression of his face adapting itself to the spirit of the psalm and with tears often coursing down his cheeks . . . yes, he sings with the very marrow of his bones, with voice, face and profound sighs, all showing how deeply he is stirred.'

In his discussions of miracles in his book *The City of God*, Augustine describes the spontaneity of the congregation in a service during Easter when two people were healed: 'Such wonder rose up from men and women together that the exclamations and tears seemed

as if they would never come to an end . . . [they] shouted
God's praises without words, but with such a noise that
our ears could scarcely stand it. What was there in the
hearts of all this clamouring crowd but the faith of
Christ . . . ?'

There are other accounts of the expressiveness of Early
Church worship. In the early fifth century a woman from
Gaul made a pilgrimage to Palestine and recorded her
experiences of Christian worship at Jerusalem in *Egeria –
the diary of a pilgrimage*. During Holy Week thousands of
people with lighted candles would retrace the steps of
Christ. Describing part of the liturgy covering the Arrest
she says: 'During the reading of the passage there is such
moaning and groaning with weeping from all the people
that their moaning can be heard practically as far as the
city.'

Eddie Ensley, who quotes many of these accounts in a
fascinating book on jubilation and expressive worship in
the Early Church, called *Sounds of Wonder**, comments:

One of the important things about the account of the
worship of the Church in Jerusalem is the way expressive prayer was tied to liturgical prayer. The response of
the people was to the hearing of the Word in a liturgical
celebration. The people were so attuned to the liturgy,
so moved by it, so open to expressing their devotion
in spontaneous ways that it was natural for them
to express their feelings in wordless sounds and
tears.

Such experience was common at this time. People prayed
with outstretched arms, clapped their hands and
laughed with joy and prostrated themselves on the
floor with remorse, whether in the liturgy, in private

* Published Paulist Press 1977.

devotions or at work out in the fields. There was a natural embracing of freedom and structure in worship.

5) Freedom Curtailed

Gradually from the fifth century this freedom became more proscribed. The fear of profane music and instruments and the weakening of true commitment, as Christianity became an accepted religion, were contributory factors. In 576 the Nectorian Synod banned the use of tambourines and castanets because of the noisy celebrations at funerals! Psaltery, tuba, drum and flute were censored for their links with war. The tibia was thought inappropriate because of its associations with orgiastic rites. Only the lyre was approved for home use. Noise and harshness were excluded from liturgical music, although more extrovert worship continued in the Eastern churches with clapping and dancing, which the Coptic Church in Ethiopia continues to this day.

These moves profoundly affected the character and development of Western music in the succeeding centuries. Many pressures bore down on congregations which made such spontaneity and spiritual sensitivity more difficult to maintain as a whole body. There were political and confessional divisions in the church while barbarian hordes made raids on society, keeping Europe in a state of disruption. More and more church music was performed by trained singers and monks.

Such leaders in worship were originally recruited from among educated laymen. These cantors adopted the practice of the Jewish synagogue. In fact many congregations used converts who had been trained there and these introduced their art into the new Christian liturgy. At first not ordained, they soon joined the ranks of the clergy as the role of singers grew in importance. Eventually monastic orders came to dominate the whole leader-

ship of the Church, and soon demanded more space in
buildings for clergy and choir alike. Special choir schools
were set up under Pope Gregory to train singers and
worship leaders. Many church dignitaries passed
through them on their way to higher office. The pro-
motion of musical art made congregational participation
in the liturgy less favourable as more and more of the
service was sung.

Melodies which had their springs in folk art and improvisation became standardised as professional choirs
perfected their performance. Such melodies became
established as Gregorian Chant and had a wide influence
on the Western Church. When primitive notation was
formulated around the eighth/ninth centuries this effectively destroyed the improvisatory quality inherent in
early Christian music. From this point improvised Jubilation ceased to be an expected part of the liturgy. This
improvised part of the 'Alleluia' came to be written down
and, because the melodies were often long and ornate,
eventually other words were written above it as an aid to
memory. In time this practice created a variety of new
musical forms including the 'sequence' and the 'trope'.

6) The Medieval Period

While Jubilation no longer held a place in the established
liturgy it was nevertheless part of the worship of groups
of ordinary people throughout the medieval period, and
among mystics until the seventeenth century. Worship
for medieval people was a personal and living thing.
There was a strong sense of devotion and the spirit of
spontaneity was maintained outside the liturgy. The
Holy Spirit was experienced as a contemporary, life-
changing force. St. Bernard spoke of this in his sermon
for Pentecost: 'The Spirit communicates itself for the
working of miracles in signs and prodigies and other

supernatural operations which he effects by the hands of whomsoever he pleases, renewing the wonders of bygone times, so that the events of the present may confirm our belief as to those of the past.'

The Liturgy reflected the inner experience of the believer. Baptism and Confirmation were merely outward signs of an inward grace. In a sermon on 'Ways that the Holy Ghost is communicated' St. Bernard speaks words that many could do with hearing today: 'We have all, I think, received the Spirit unto salvation, but not to all has he been given unto fervour. In fact, very few show any desire to obtain it. We are content with our own cramped littleness, and make no endeavour to rejoice in or at least aspire to the liberty of spirit which that Spirit confers.'

The zeal of the Holy Spirit was expressed in practical action. Monasteries were centres of art and learning, but also of love and compassion in caring for the needy. The building of cathedrals was just one example of this powerful dynamic of faith in men's hearts. Doubtless some were built for worldly glory, but some, like Chartres, were built in times of great religious revival. Here, thousands of voluntary workers, gathered from rich and poor alike, joined together to raise this magnificent structure to the glory of God. Work on the cathedral was seen as a religious act requiring men to attend confession and to put right grudges and hostilities towards each other. Many were brought to new faith as a result. During the building many sick were prayed for, and spontaneous praise and worship would break out as people sang psalms and hymns and prayed with fervour.

7) Divorce Proceedings

Meanwhile a divorce from pure liturgical aims had already begun in music. Through the control of the Church over all artistic matters, Western music was almost exclusively identified with the music of the liturgy. Musicians began to experience a conflict of loyalties. They desired to serve and enhance the liturgy with their music but at the same time wished to develop their musical skills freely. Personal and professional ambition began to pull against the restriction which philosophy and liturgy had laid down. Albert Seay wrote:

> With the advancing thirteenth century, the paths of philosophers and musicians began to diverge. Where adjustments of the one to the needs of the other had previously been made without effort and with alacrity, there were now increasing indications of a basic split in the understanding of a common goal . . . In music, the liturgy and its embellishment no longer had overpowering interest for the composer; his concern with the development of technique was now more and more for its own sake.*

This new period in art became known as the 'Ars Nova'. There was much innovation and, as if to emphasise its new independence, instrumental music previously held in suspicion by the Church Fathers began to be introduced into musical art. Composers still provided great sacred masterpieces for the use of the Church but their centre of interest and activity lay beyond its walls. Congregational needs and participation in the music of the liturgy had long since been dismissed and was only later rediscovered by the reforms of Luther and his friends who restored some life and dignity to congregational music.

As for 'art' music, the Church never recovered its control. Composers wrote for its liturgy, but apart from a few, like J. S. Bach, their main creative focus was else-

* Source: Albert Seay, *Music in the Medieval World*, Prentice-Hall History of Music Series, 1965.

where. In the seventeenth and eighteenth centuries, church music borrowed the styles and affectations of the princely courts and glorified the pomp and ceremony of man rather than God. Religious revivals amongst ordinary people, such as the Wesleyan revival in the eighteenth century, resulted in a burst of creative energy in hymn writing, for example, but did not affect musical art in general. In the nineteenth century the idea of the great composer reached its apotheosis as the lonely artist struggled to express his identity in the middle of a hostile universe. Sacred art was seen as grave and archaic with little joy or vitality. A mock-religiosity prevailed.

Our own time has seen the decline of a whole musical culture in Western music. The main cultural and creative streams in music today have come from outside Europe – Africa, America and the East. The people, alienated from 'art' music, have formulated their own pervasive musical expression. How interesting that 'pop' music had its springs in Christian worship – the Black Gospel music of the American slaves.

8) Rediscovering Roots

In the midst of a period of enormous change, the Church is changing too. It has not been immune to popular grassroots movements. Huge changes have been accomplished in liturgical renewal, particularly in the Roman Catholic Church. These are no less significant than the challenge of the Charismatic renewal to rediscover the present work and gifts of the Holy Spirit.

Both are in perfect step with the ancient tradition and practice of the Church. Through contemporary renewal, music is rediscovering its role in worship. New music is being created, not just by professional musicians, but by the people, for the people. Similarly, the improvising of music in worship is recapturing the ethos and spirit of its ancient roots. People are discovering that what is often called 'traditional' is in fact profoundly out of step with the true traditions of Christianity. Rather than seeing current renewal movements as unique and without precedent, the experience of free and expressive worship through many centuries of Church history offers those involved in renewal today a new sense of balance and perspective, authenticity and dignity. Those suspicious or frightened by aspects of contemporary renewal movements can be reassured where these are in harmony with the experience of the past. Christian renewal is in fact always a rediscovery of Biblical and Spiritual roots. Ensley sums this up:

> When the Church pushed the panic button at the Council of Trent, much of the flow of tradition began to stop. In many areas such as Scripture, spirituality and liturgy the Church lost vital contact with its sources. The liturgical and Biblical movements that led to Vatican Council II have opened the door again to tradition so that the Church can creatively face its future by drawing on the richness of its past.*

The church musician today is faced with the challenge of matching these tremendous and exciting changes in liturgical spiritual renewal, with music that adequately expresses the faith and worship of a new and dynamic Church. Perhaps in the process he will become the prophet of a God-given gift to a society whose music seems to revolve in ever decreasing circles!

* Source: Eddie Ensley 'Sounds Of Wonder', published by Paulist Press.

2

THE MEANING OF WORSHIP

1) What is Worship?

Karl Barth wrote that 'Christian worship is the most momentous, the most urgent, the most glorious action that can take place in human life.' Good for Karl Barth you might say, but he hasn't been to my church! How often our worship falls short of the ideals we hold. Theologians come up with great and lofty statements, others revise services to enshrine them, but at All Hallows in the Marshes, things grind on in the form that they have always taken. Somehow, directives from the top never change things because people themselves haven't changed.

Liturgical reform, new and more approachable styles of music, restructured buildings, all can aid worship; but they can never provide that intimate spark that touches off the love and adoration of each individual's heart and which, when blended together in the Body of Christ, begins to express the presence of Christ among his people. To modify a quote: 'Worship which does not begin with the individual, does not begin.' Whatever our vision for worship, it must begin with me, in my heart.

At the heart of worship is a personal knowledge of God. You cannot have worship without faith. In Acts 17:22 St. Paul, speaking to the men of Athens says: 'I perceive that in every way you are very religious, for as I passed along and observed the objects of your worship, I found also an altar with the inscription: "To an unknown God." What therefore you worship as unknown, this I proclaim to you.'

We worship whom we know. We know God through Jesus Christ whose 'love has been poured into our hearts through the Holy Spirit'. This has been given to each believer to confirm and make real their faith. Without a personal experience of Jesus and the receiving of his Spirit, we are like the Athenians worshipping an unknown God. How can there be vitality and renewal in worship unless the Holy Spirit has first wakened the spirit of worship in each one of us personally? How can our music ever truly express our faith? We may sing all the right songs, raise our hands, do all the right things, but never be able to echo the words of the psalmist: 'How I love *you* Lord!' (Ps. 18:1)

2) The Word 'Worship'

Our English word 'worship' comes from the Anglo-Saxon *weorthscipe* – to attribute worth to something. Worship therefore has everything to do with what we value in life. Man has always had an instinctive need to worship, whether in the primitive tribes of New Guinea or in our own technological society. We just have different names for our gods. In fact, it's not a matter of 'Do you worship?'; more 'What do you worship?' In primitive societies men worshipped the things that gave and sustained life: the sun and moon, the earth and the spirits of forest and river. Indeed, the whole of life was regarded as a sacred act which engaged man's whole being in symbols, gestures, drama, song and dance. Also, his worship was communal as he saw himself as just one part of the whole.

Today we worship other gods with no less fervour. These are more subtle, sophisticated idols involving our attitudes and desires more than wood or stone. Our gods are the gods of money, possessions, career, personal pleasure, relationships, even 'footbaal', as a friend of mine calls it. Religious observance and the music we provide for it can all too easily join the list.

But we have also lost our corporate identity and that close contact with the rhythms of life which our ancestors had. We are more like Roman society, recklessly pursuing sensuous pleasures, of whom St. Paul wrote: 'For although they knew God, they neither glorified him, nor gave thanks to him . . . They exchanged the truth about God for a lie and worshipped and served created things rather than the Creator . . . Therefore God gave them up . . .' (Rom. 1:21–24)

In other words, if you don't worship the Creator, you will end up worshipping the creature in one form or another.

To worship God is therefore to give God his worth: 'Worthy art thou O Lord our God to receive glory and honour and power, for thou didst create all things and by thy will they existed and were created' (Rev. 4:11).

In Hebrew there are several words used where we use only one to express the meaning of 'worship'. Of these, two are the most common.

The first is *Shachah*, or words related to its root, and this means bowing down before God in deep humility and respect. Two obvious references from the Old Testament would be:

Ps. 95:6 – 'O come let us worship and *bow down*, let us kneel before the Lord our Maker.'
and 1 Chr. 16:29 – 'Worship the Lord in the beauty of holiness' – other translations: 'Bow down to the Lord . . .'

As we draw near in worship, we begin to realise the greatness and power of God: 'O Lord, our Lord, how majestic is thy name in all the earth' (Ps. 8:1). He is the 'high and lofty One who inhabits eternity, whose name is Holy' (Isa. 57:15). As Christians, we can sometimes be very casual about our relationship with God and it's good to remember that, although he shows us a personal human face in Jesus, he is still 'our Maker'. Isaiah continues: 'I dwell in the high and holy place and also with him who is of a contrite and humble spirit.'

Understanding God's greatness and holiness leads us to acknowledge our own sin and weakness; also the limitations of our minds to comprehend his thoughts or his ways. The Holy Spirit is a *Holy* Spirit. We can often equate 'spirit filled' worship with exuberance and enthusiasm, how much excitement we are getting from it, but maybe not much with quietness and reverence. The hymn says: 'Let all mortal flesh keep silence, and with fear and trembling stand.' Our 'flesh' can so easily overtake us in such worship, not only in lively, extrovert situations, but also where we may exalt beauty and art, thinking that this too constitutes worship. In both instances the Spirit of God quietly recedes from our midst. A bowing down in our spirits as we approach God keeps us humble and is an important ingredient of true and spiritual worship.

Many things can touch off the spirit of worship – it is by no means restricted to church buildings. Someone said: 'The essence of worship is wonder.' There are many times in life when a beautiful thing in nature – perhaps a sunset, a flower, the vastness of space, a moment of human love when spirits touch in a beautiful way – can cause us to bow down inwardly before a greater power at work than ourselves. Ps. 46:10 – 'Be still and know that I am God. I am exalted among the nations, I am exalted in the earth'.

The second Hebrew word often used to express the idea of worship is *Abad*. This means 'service', the kind of service given by slaves or hired servants. Worship implies a total surrender of our whole lives to God as slaves in his service. Christ, in Luke 17:7–10 warned us not to be presumptuous about our service of God and expect to take our ease as a right. The slave came in from a hard day's work in the fields but had to prepare his master's food before he could look to himself. In the Hebrew mind there was no distinction between serving God and worshipping him. Thus we read in Psalm 100 'Make a joyful noise to the Lord, all the lands! Serve the Lord with gladness! Come into his presence with singing!'

Ps. 116 brings out the servant analogy even more distinctly:

'O Lord, I am thy servant, the son of thy handmaid. Thou hast loosed my bonds, I will offer to thee the sacrifice of thanksgiving and call on the name of the Lord' (v. 16).

Jesus brought together the two ideas of submission and service which *Schachah* and *Abad* express in his summary of the law and commandments:

Luke 10:25 'You shall love the Lord your God with all your heart, soul, mind and strength . . .'
but also: 'You shall love your neighbour as yourself.'

He put this love into action by making himself the servant of his disciples and washing their feet at the Last Supper. Worship must always have a practical out-working in everyday life if it is to have integrity and depth. Jesus heightened and developed the traditional Jewish view of worship by introducing a personal love relationship with God as *Abba* – Father. He made the service of God and others much more practical and radical as the out-working of that love.

3) Intimate Worship

In the New Testament the word most commonly used for worship is *Proskuneo*. Basically, it means to 'come towards to kiss'. It is most commonly used where adoration is implied such as in the worship of heaven described in the Book of Revelation. It is used to translate Jesus' words in John 4:23, 'The true worshippers will worship the Father in spirit and in truth, for such the Father seeks to worship him.' Jesus' whole ministry was to reveal God as a loving, heavenly father who desires the love and devotion of human hearts more than outward obeisance and ritual. In the New Testament the word *Abba* is used to address God and this is an Aramaic word which a child would use for his father or 'daddy'. St. Paul uses it in Romans 8:15 – 'When we cry "Abba! Father!" it is the Spirit himself bearing witness with our spirit that we are children of God.'

Both are intimate words of love and reflect the new relationship which we are able to have with God through Jesus Christ. Instead of needing a priest or mediator, we may now enter fully into his presence, not in cringing fear, but knowing that we are totally forgiven and made righteous through his sacrifice on the cross. This should deeply affect our attitude towards worship. Our acceptability does not depend on our worthiness. True, we must be honest about our sin and weakness, but, having confessed it, we are to cast it aside and enter in. We are not to hover on the threshold with feelings of guilt and unworthiness. As George Herbert wrote: 'Love bade me welcome but my soul drew back, guiltie of duste and sinne.'

So much of our freedom in worship is hindered by such feelings. Like the prodigal son, we find it hard to accept the father's unconditional love and make a free offering of love in return. Perhaps it is a fear of what others, like the elder brother in the parable, may feel.

For some there is no intimacy in worship. Worship is a legal duty that God requires of us and if we can make it as beautiful and perfect as humanly possible then it will be acceptable. There is much in this approach to commend it. God should receive our very best in worship, whatever 'best' means for us. But much more important is our attitude of heart. God says in Amos: 'This people honours me with their lips but their heart is far from me.' Our worship may be the most beautiful offering – the choir's diction and tone impeccable, the setting perfect – but if we remain cold and detached and do not offer God the personal devotion of our hearts, how can it be acceptable? Our worship has had more to do with the Old Testament than the New. We are to be in love with Jesus.

To love somebody deeply, you must know them as fully as you can. To worship intimately depends on a personal knowledge of God, but it also depends on being able to express that love. A marriage is more than a verbal contract, it must be consummated – the love must be expressed physically and emotionally: 'With my body I thee worship.' To worship God at all we need the Holy Spirit to enable us to cry 'Abba! Father!' But for worship to express our love fully to God with all that we have we require the power of the Spirit to release our emotions. We must be filled with the Spirit. As George T. Montague put it: 'Can we say it more simply? Lovers have many ways of expressing their love, but especially two. One is the words "I love you". The other is the kiss. God's word to me, reduced to essence, is "I love you". His Spirit, as the mystics long ago observed, is his kiss.' Being filled with the Spirit therefore is to allow oneself to be 'kissed' and embraced by God.

4) The Breadth of Worship

From the variety of words used to express the idea of worship in the Bible, we can see that worship is meant to be all-inclusive. It covers the whole of life. As Amos reminds us, God is not just interested in what we may say or sing with our lips in church on a Sunday, but more particularly with the kind of people we are day by day.

We frequently live as divided people in two separate worlds: the sacred and the secular. In the sacred compartment we keep God, the Bible, prayer, Christian fellowship, good works. In another, much bigger compartment, we keep our family, possessions, money, ambition, career, pleasure, relationships . . . and ne'er the twain shall meet!

On the surface we appear to be very committed Christians attending meetings, praying and studying the Bible, but, in fact, we are really only serving ourselves. Most of the time, except for our words, there is little to distinguish us from the rest of the world. We have the same values as anybody else – new car, holiday in Spain, video etc., and we get just as cross and self-righteous when someone does us down. What we assent to in church, like submitting to God and loving our neighbour, gets no further than the church door. Our worship is really no more than lip-service to God.

Someone once said; 'As much as you worship God in your daily life is as much as you worship God!' This is a sobering thought indeed and I expect, if we are honest, we would have to say that we actually worship God very little at all. Most of the time we are only really interested in and preoccupied with ourselves! What do you find your thoughts turning to when you wake up in the morning, drive to work, push the hoover around? These are often the things we worship in reality.

God wants us to be unified, whole people. He cares for

our spirits, but he also cares for our minds and bodies and what we do with them. Nothing that we do or think is beyond the scope of his love. It therefore matters to him what we do with our money, whom we marry, where we go on holiday or what our attitudes are towards other people. When we open these areas to the Lordship of Christ, they too become worship. In fact a much deeper, more real worship than what goes on in church. This should only be the outward expression of lives totally submitted and committed to the service of God. The sacred area of life, rather than be trapped in its safe compartment, is then able to release its power into the secular area. We begin to pray when we face a difficult decision at work or when we need someone to collect the children from school because we can't cope ourselves. We read the Bible and expect God to speak to us for that particular day. Maybe we carry a particular verse with us to meditate on during the day.

To bring worship into our everyday lives is to learn to praise God at every opportunity. Singing simple songs of worship or joining in with a tape while we are doing the chores can lift our spirits enormously, even carry us through a difficult or irksome task. Alternatively, we can exercise the gift of tongues if we have received it. St. Paul said: 'He who speaks in a tongue edifies himself' (1 Cor. 14:4). This gift is a way of communing with God deep within our spirit without needing to concentrate in our mind. It re-establishes our relationship with our Heavenly Father – another way of crying 'Abba! Father!' as his children. It is not an ecstatic gift and can be exercised or terminated at will. No special feelings are required to begin and its use will make us sensitive to the Holy Spirit and open a door to other gifts.

5) The Power of Worship

Richard Foster, in his book *Celebration of Discipline* says: 'To stand before the Holy One of Eternity is to change.' To worship is to change. In Romans 12:1 we read: 'Do not be conformed to this world, *but be transformed by the renewal of your mind.*'

Jesus, the Light of the World, was a pure, transparent and perfect life – a life that worshipped God completely in body, mind and spirit. Like Jesus, God wants us more and more to become whole people in order that we may worship him fully. Rather than a negative, restricting thing, worship becomes liberating and transforming. It touches each part of life and its light permeates into the dark and closed corners of our beings.

In Ephesians 5:8 we read: 'Once you were darkness, but now you are light in the Lord; walk as children of light . . . When anything is exposed by the light, it becomes visible, for anything that becomes visible is light.'

Whatever darkness there is within us, it can be opened up to God's light to become light as it is transformed by his power. Holding ourselves in the light and allowing God to change us is therefore the place of true worship. It is allowing Jesus to be Lord of all that we are. It requires *honesty* about our own sin and weakness and the ability to admit that we are really not as perfect as we make out. It requires *openness* to allow the Holy Spirit to search out every dark area within us. *Perseverance* too is needed to see things through to the end and not 'flip out' when God is just about to complete the change in us. Most of all we need a sense of *hope* that it is possible to change at all and be free from our old selves.

There was once a caterpillar talking to a friend when a beautiful butterfly lurched precariously by. 'Huh,' said the caterpillar, 'You'll never get me up in one of those things!'

Of course the caterpillar's whole existence was geared to attaining the freedom and beauty of the butterfly, but he didn't fancy the risk. Very often we would rather stick where we are, maybe feeling trapped or depressed at the kind of people we are, but at least safe. We prefer our old suit of clothes. When God offers us a new one, we say 'Thank you very much' and keep it in the wardrobe for Sundays! This is not what God intends for us and we will soon find that, rather than remaining safe and secure, we are in fact becoming hard and withdrawn.

Allowing God to become the centre and focus of our lives is a painful process. 'Men love the darkness rather than the light because their deeds are evil.' He will frequently use our fellow Christians to reveal our sin and help us change and grow. I lived in a community for six years and found it one of the most fruitful and growing periods of my life. Through living closely with one another we quickly got to know what sort of people we really were. This wasn't usually a very spiritual exercise. It happened when one person reacted to another constantly leaving the top off the toothpaste, or not closing the front door! Very often you would begin putting somebody right about their shortcomings only to end up asking forgiveness yourself.

The encouraging thing was that your love for the other person grew a little bit more each time and *you* changed a little too. Such confrontations were called 'walking in the light' – occasions that we didn't look forward to, but which always bore fruit in our lives. St. John talks about this in 1 John 1:7. Notice that it is in the context of love and forgiveness through Christ that such honesty is possible. His love sets the context for the light to shine.

Worship can only be as deep, as broad, as free or as joyful as we are. God's power is available to change us – but are we willing to allow him to begin?

6) Corporate Worship

Someone said that the church reminded them of a bus – a driver up at the front who determined direction, all the passengers arranged passively in serried ranks behind, and even someone to come round and collect the fares!

In a huge number of churches the minister is left to do everything – preach, teach, counsel, organise, even put out the chairs and sometimes play the organ too! No wonder many of them succeed in doing nothing well – except having nervous breakdowns and marriage break-ups. No wonder many congregations are dissatisfied with the whole situation. I heard of one church that decided to do something about it and instituted a special chain letter. This is what it said:

'If you are unhappy with your vicar, simply have your churchwardens send a copy of this letter to six other churches who are also tired of their vicar. Then bundle up your vicar and send him to the church at the top of the list. Within a week you will receive 16,435 vicars, one of which should at least be acceptable. (Have faith in this chain-letter, do not break the chain – one church did and got their old vicar back!)'

How are you getting on with your minister? Alternatively, how is he or she getting on with you? Sadly, there is little idea of corporateness in many churches. Instead of a living body with each member working properly together, the church so often operates a one-man show; and this with the complicity of the congregation who find it more convenient to employ one person to look after their spiritual affairs than take responsibility themselves.

In worship it's just the same. Here the Organist Rules O.K.! He is the one-man band, the master of all musical resources which he holds captive in one enormous box. Between them, vicar and organist can have a stranglehold on most areas of church life.

Instead, worship is intended to be corporate. It is to be a rich and varied reflection of the whole of life brought in as an offering of thanksgiving to God, not something dull and monochrome. In Romans 12:1 we read: 'Present your bodies as a living sacrifice, holy and acceptable, which is your spiritual worship.'

We, as many *bodies*, combine to offer to the Lord *one* living sacrifice. Worship, therefore, implies relationships. As Christians, we worship the relationship of the Trinity – Father, Son and Spirit. In John 17, Jesus invites us to share in that relationship as children of God: 'My prayer is that you be of one heart and mind and that you share my glory, the glorious unity of being one as we are.' (Living Bible).

The corporate nature of the Godhead is thus most perfectly worshipped in a corporate way. In 1 Peter 2:5 the Church is pictured as made up of 'living stones' built into a spiritual temple in which spiritual sacrifices are offered to God. We are to be interdependent, like stones in a building, each one indispensable, each one chiselled and moulded to fit perfectly with the others in exactly its right place.

Throughout history, God has been forming a people to worship him – a community of love which reflects his nature and expresses his character. The idea of community is hard for us to understand in Western society. We all try to be independent and self-sufficient. In fact, the sense of community is breaking down altogether in many places and society is becoming increasingly fragmented with people alienated from one another.

Many of us come into God's new community from this background and have to learn a completely new way of relating. We know we should be loving, committed, trusting towards each other, but somehow we can't work it out. We are like porcupines on a cold night huddling together for warmth but instantly recoiling as soon as we prick and hurt each other!

Nevertheless, the worship of a loving and unified community of Christians is the deepest that we can experience outside of heaven – and it is what God intended for us. John in his first Epistle wrote: 'No man has ever seen God; if we love one another, God abides in us and his love is perfected in us' (4:12). Staggering words indeed! An important part of worship is, therefore, to live in love with our brothers and sisters.

Some would not see it this way. In a *Daily Telegraph* magazine article of a few years ago, the precentor of a certain English cathedral was quoted as follows: 'White-haired, benign, he stopped to light a cigarette in his house in the Close. Outside, the red-stone bulk of the cathedral rose against the sky. "You can imagine it at 5.30 on a February evening," said the Canon dreamily, "the ice and snow on the ground. Inside there is a perfect gem of an evensong and nobody there at all to listen to it. Nobody. This is worship at its most perfect."'

Aesthetically beautiful, no doubt, but 'worship at its

most perfect' (partly because there are no common
people around to sully it) – surely not! No, spiritual
sacrifices acceptable to God through Jesus Christ have
everything to do with the integrity of the lives that offer
them and how those lives are built together into a temple
made with living stones.

Another definition has a more New Testament ring
about it: 'Worship is loving God in the presence of one
another and loving one another in the presence of God.'
Someone with great authority to write about the essence
of corporate worship because of her deep involvement
in Christian community, is the composer and music
director Betty Pulkingham. She writes:

> What after all, constitutes beauty in worship? Is it to be
> measured by an aesthetic yardstick (how flawlessly the
> choir sings, how eloquent the preacher) or is it the
> measuring rod of a much finer and more sensitive
> dimension, discernable only by the Spirit of God?
> Romans 12 unlocks the key to understanding spiritual
> worship as an offering of our bodies, living sacrifices,
> holy, pleasing to God. Corporate worship is that hap-
> pening, however simply achieved, where all are made
> to feel a part of the whole, and the whole is given to
> God – a simple enough formula, but certainly not one
> that is achieved without a great deal of effort, vigilance
> and caring on the part of those who are leaders in
> worship.*

When we gather together in worship, we are told in
Ephesians and the other Epistles, that all the fullness of
Christ dwells among us, with all his power to change,
heal and free us. In this, every member of the Body of
Christ is indispensable and without each member's

---

* From an article in 'Music in Worship' Magazine Dec. 1980.

active participation, that presence is lessened. The gifts of the Holy Spirit are the living movements of the Body of Christ, as Dr. James Dunn expressed it, and it is these gifts that minister God's life to his people and to the world.

This last point is worth expanding. We receive God's gifts in worship, not just for ourselves but, perhaps more importantly, for others. Worship can never be a selfish thing – how can it be, if we are really surrendering all we have to God? The Church is called to be a sign of God's Kingdom in the world, and in worship we proclaim this more significantly than in anything else. Our unity and love speaks more eloquently than a thousand sermons, anthems or hymns! In John 13, Jesus says: 'A new commandment I give to you, that you love one another: even as I have loved you, that you also love one another. By this all men will know that you are my disciples, if you have love for one another.'

7) Family Worship

As we learn to love and accept one another in the Body of Christ, worship begins to become an intimate 'family' experience. It becomes a place to be real and honest; to take off the masks of self-sufficiency, of being able to cope, and to share our weakness so that God's power can take over. A family is made up of young and old, people of different tastes and interests, but they all have a blood relationship whatever they may be feeling towards one another at the time. They don't have to pretend to be accepted.

We are members of God's family, but God's love is sterile and meaningless unless expressed in human terms. God didn't send a book of instructions down from heaven and tell us to get on with it – he sent a living human person to demonstrate his love and to show us what a life in total communion with God could be like. Jesus was the Word of God made flesh. We, today, are his Body and must similarly 'enflesh' that same life.

Most of God's gifts of love and grace are expressed towards us through our brothers and sisters in that family. We need one another in order to become the whole and mature Christ-like people God means us to be.

Worshipping as members of the same family teaches us much about ourselves and about others. As we worship we lay ourselves open to God and to one another. The Spirit begins to soften and melt some of the hard and frozen areas in our lives which shut us off from him and one another. We begin to be really ourselves, with all our faults and failings, and, in turn, our worship becomes more real. People begin to sense God's presence among us in almost tangible ways, not only in services, but whenever we meet together. Even in a formal setting, newcomers are not excluded by a stiff religiosity, but feel welcomed in. At the other extreme, the frothy shallowness of much so-called 'charismatic' worship is replaced by the integrity and strength of deep and committed relationships and a new freedom of the whole person. All sorts of people are drawn into such worship, even children, who can so often detect when something is false, take their place.

A quote from *Declare His Praise – an introduction to Family Worship* from the Community of Celebration admirably sums it up:

The Spirit is stirring the church to a new awareness of itself as the Family of God. Many churches are becoming places where people feel at home with each other. Members of the church are beginning to share at many levels: their abilities, their concerns, their time, their families. They are finding their basic needs being met by each other. Their worship then becomes an extension of this deepened human sharing . . .

This sense of being 'at home' also liberates creativity to renew worship. In an accepting environment, a timid musician may find courage to contribute his music, a dancer may create a new dance of praise, a writer may develop readings and prayers to express the heart and mind of the family at a particular time. Persons who felt they had nothing to give may find new abilities emerge to their surprise and delight. Children are drawn into the sense of family and offer their own gifts of spontaneity and joy. Worship begins to embody the warmth and tenderness of a family occasion.

3

PREPARING TO WORSHIP

In the previous chapter we looked at the meaning of worship. In this chapter I would like to look at how that worship can be expressed in both formal and informal settings. We have over the years learnt the value of worship in both these areas – in our public services and in house and fellowship meetings. We have also tried to integrate them and break down some of the sharp divisions that have existed between traditional and contemporary approaches. It has not been an easy balance to maintain, but the tension has been very creative in our expression of worship.

For us, the renewal of the Spirit in personal lives as well as church structures has combined with the ethos of a beautiful medieval church and some classical orientation in music to produce a depth, integrity and gentleness in worship which is particularly striking. Hundreds of people from many traditions have visited us to experience the life of the church and have felt at home in our worship. Somehow we have managed to draw together many strands from the different traditions to make something new.

Through our desire to communicate personally with believer and non-believer alike we have developed our own 'folk' art. Like our people it is constantly changing, growing and evolving, summing up our life and experience, our joys and battles, our suffering too. It is 'people's' art, not pretentious, trying to be better than it is, but instead genuinely representing the feelings and aspirations of our people through a combination of many styles and varieties of expression.

The art forms we employ are basically congregational, particularly in the music, with a high degree of participation and spontaneity. By 'folk' art I do not mean wailing singers, amateur accordion players or quaint country dancing! We could equally employ a traditional hymn or prayer or a classical piece of music. The vital condition is whether or not it is really 'owned' by the people. Is it something in which they can feel comfortable and at home? Can they be themselves in all the richness and variety which that implies?

We are always looking for ways in which to draw people in and give them the opportunity to offer themselves and their gifts in worship. Many people write their own songs, make banners or create new dances for example. In this way they interpret the present activity of the Spirit among us and provide avenues of communication between God and one another.

Worship is not just a spiritual activity. We are offering the whole of ourselves to God. In Christianity the spiritual and earthly are inextricably linked with one another. Spiritual gifts have ordinary, human façades. The sacraments take their meaning from earthly, mundane things given special significance by the touch of the Holy Spirit: the bread and wine in communion, the water of baptism or the laying on of hands in prayer. Worship too is prepared by human hands, minds and bodies – an offering transformed by the presence of God. Everything about it is ordinary and natural, especially its imperfections, but somehow we meet with God and are inwardly changed.

The following pages represent some of the things we have learnt, seeking to summarise and interpret what the Spirit has been doing among us week by week.

ONE: FORMAL WORSHIP

1) The Form of Worship

'A service is the creation of an atmosphere in which
a spiritual miracle may take place.'

Most corporate worship is offered in the form of a
service of one kind or another. In it people set aside a
particular time and place where they can concentrate
their minds and wills in the company of others and make
their offering of worship to God. These occasions take on
a wide variety of forms in the Christian Church but share
common ingredients. They may be as highly organised as
Choral Evensong or as joyfully chaotic as a Family Service. Even the most informal meeting like a house fellowship has some kind of organisation and a familiar
progression of ingredients.

A service helps to unify us and lead us together into the
presence of God. In it the life of the church is focused in a
public expression on one particular occasion. It may
consist of:
- Worship, praise and thanksgiving.
- Proclaiming the Kingdom of God and Jesus as Lord.
- Expressing identity as the people of God.
- Giving opportunity for teaching, encouragement,
  communication.
- Making a summary of our whole life together as the
  Body of Christ.

This ordering of our public worship is called 'Liturgy'.
It comes from the original Greek *Leitourgia* combining the
words *Laos* (people) and *Ergon* (work).

A 'liturgy' in Ancient Greek society was literally 'a work done for the people'. A rich person might pay the cost of providing a bridge or a road for the public good. It's easy to see why the word was picked up in the context of worship. Providing a liturgy for an act of worship is like building a bridge or a road. Like a bridge, it links different sides together over a natural division. Like a road, it gathers people together and enables them to pass along easily in a common direction.

Liturgy is the mechanics of public worship. It is the stones, girders, nuts and bolts which support and sustain it. These raw materials are different according to the type of community and the resources which they represent, just as some bridges are old, some new, some very humble, while others span great estuaries. Usually however, they will consist of ingredients such as preaching, teaching, prayer, symbolic actions (processing or raising hands), meditation and of course the arts, such as music. There are many more.

The art of liturgy is achieving a balance between all these different elements and making them alive and relevant to the participants. It is sensitive to people's tastes and needs. It also understands what is happening to people's minds, emotions, wills and spirits during a service, not in a clinical, calculating way, but in order to ensure a fulfilling experience of worship within a limited time. Planning liturgy involves imagining people's responses, how they will interpret the different elements and make sense of them.

Often this is left to the vicar or minister alone. He chooses the hymns and prayers to fit in with the lectionary reading for the day or perhaps a particular theme he wants to expound. If he does his work properly he prepares in advance and lets the musicians and others know in good time. If not, he skims through the hymn or prayer book five minutes before and picks at random items which may have no relevance or inter-relationship whatsoever.

Those who plan liturgy have a great responsibility and an almost impossible task!

2) Planning Worship

In St. Michael's, when worship was still a 'hymn-sandwich' and the organist unco-operative, the vicar used to choose all the hymns. Although he did a reasonable job and even kept a chart of when they had been used, he inevitably had fairly limited tastes. When I became organist we took the bold step of choosing them together. This made the process a little more representative, but it wasn't until the worship became more creative and varied, with the introduction of new songs, dances and other art forms, that we decided to form a planning group. We called it the Worship Committee and it has continued in roughly the same form down to the present day.

By having a group to plan our services we hoped to make them more balanced and representative. Such a group would be made up of people from different areas within the life of the congregation but with a particular interest in worship. They needed to be people who could talk out what God was saying and doing within the church at that moment and find the elements which could best interpret this. Practically, they needed time to meet together and to have a positive input.

Today the Worship Committee consists of clergy, director of music, and representatives from choir, dance and banner groups and the children's work. Recently, we have expanded our horizons by encouraging other groups to take responsibility for planning some of the services. This has increased people's sense of responsibility and identity with the worship. A representative will join us to report back. Occasionally, we set up a resource group from many areas in the church's life to examine the whole of our worship life and to feed in comments, criticisms and suggestions.

The aim of the committee is to plan the form and content of our Sunday services from themes and readings chosen by the pastorate of the church. It meets once a week and is generally planning a fortnight ahead to give resource groups such as the choir, time to prepare their material. Sometimes it looks further ahead to special festivals or celebrations which need more preparation.

It is mainly involved in choosing musical items as these make up the major proportion of ingredients under its control. The non-musical members are able to bring a lot of ordinary, objective input from their vantage point in the pew. We also incorporate dance or short pieces of drama and try to weave everything together with a common thread. All the different ingredients are seen as part of the whole, each revealing a different facet of the theme we are seeking to develop. Each part also represents the different areas of our life as the family of God in which each age-group has equal right to a voice.

Our tasks include talking over the Sunday before, *evaluating* what went well, whether the ingredients were appropriate, which parts went badly – through ill preparation or bad planning – and what could be learnt for the future. Sometimes this is just for our benefit, but at other times it is important for the participants to have constructive feed-back so that ministries may develop and mature.

Prayer is important because we are planning for maximum involvement and maximum response to what we believe God is wanting to do and say. To achieve this we need the Spirit's help to inspire our minds and imaginations and fulfil his will through our common agreement as well as the occasional disagreement. Through prayer we submit ourselves to one another and to God. Much of what we do revolves around our own particular tastes and it is very easy to polarise into different camps, each with its own idea of what should be done. We can soon forget that we are there to serve the congregation, not our own preferences. For example, we may not personally like a particular song or dance but it may identify with a certain section of the congregation and therefore be justified. A prayerful attitude assures that we remain open to the Spirit and to each other.

Selecting the different elements involves *submission* and 'preferring one another in love' (Rom. 12:10). This is why our group is such an excellent vehicle for planning corporate worship and why its efforts are often so appropriate to the occasion. Many times people have mentioned how a hymn, song or drama has spoken to them and echoed just what they were feeling, even though it may have been planned a couple of weeks before. It seems that God inspires and directs us as we try to operate in a small way like the Body of Christ itself.

3) Guidelines in Worship

The ordering and presenting of our public worship requires skill and understanding to make it work. Of course we never stop learning. It is impossible to organise and structure the Holy Spirit!

From the painful and breathless experience of ceaselessly trying to catch up with God, I would like to develop five main areas for consideration as we plan more formal worship. I hope they will have relevance to all churches of whatever background.

i) **Communication:** David Watson's guiding principle in his ministry was **relevance**! In every service, particularly when evangelistic and for the outsider, he would examine each constituent part, whether hymn, reading, prayer or sermon, to see if it related to and was understood by ordinary people. Each part had to have a reason for being there and needed to complement the whole. Dead wood was ruthlessly cut out to streamline the impact of whatever theme or message was to be communicated. Needless to say, the services became very powerful means of communication in which the sermon was the climax.

We try to apply the same principles today. Our worship has improved enormously in quality and variety since those early days, but the need to keep relevant and in touch with the people in the pews is as vital as ever. The sermon is still extremely important for us, but the focus now rests on the atmosphere of worship, love and freedom experienced in the service as a whole.

As planners of our services we are there to help people worship and communicate with God. The different ingredients need to serve that end. Each part must be balanced sensitively with the others to produce a sense of flow and climax. Simplicity and clarity in words and music is vital – we avoid hymns with obscure or sentimental language for example. The service-leader is encouraged to host the service, not speaking with a special 'churchy' voice in a detached or impersonal manner, but being natural, warm and able to make people feel relaxed. Good links and introductions between the different items can help to smooth out the bumps and open up the theme, interpreting the direction of the service so that people feel secure and involved. These should be short and clear. The songs and hymns should link into the theme or readings for the day. They give opportunity for people to reflect on or respond to the different parts of the service and should not continually be introducing new themes at a tangent to the whole.

Each service is different and we should never assume that what worked one week will do again for the next;

each time we are provided with a unique opportunity to
meet with God. As we plan with prayer, we are providing pathways for people to open up to him so that he may
work. The natural progression of ingredients within a
service reflects our relationship with God: we begin with
confession, we praise God for our forgiveness, we thank
him for his love and faithfulness, we pray about our
needs and concerns, we hear his word and in turn
respond.

If we ignore this dynamic we are likely to get into
trouble. Praise may not lift off if people have not had the
opportunity to put themselves right with God and with
one another in confession. A teaching at the beginning of
a meeting may find people still cold and unresponsive
and unable to hear the Lord. Starting the service with a
quiet meditative hymn may not provide sufficient grip
to gather people up and focus their concentration. They
may need a strong, positive one instead.

What of the length of services? A service that overruns
its time on a Sunday morning is unlikely to encourage
free, undistracted worship. All the ladies in the congregation will begin to wonder whether the lunch is burning!
Longer services do not guarantee greater depth or freedom in worship either. God is able to work 'in the
twinkling of an eye'!

Each service will have a different *focus* and it is important to know what this is as it is planned. In some services it may be teaching, in others praise or celebration.
Sometimes a service may have testimony or an evangelistic presentation as its main thrust. The planning
group should seek the mind of the Spirit in this – what
does God want to say or do through this service? We can
easily try to develop too many threads and cause confusion or frustration. Holy Communion has a clear focus
because everything progresses towards the central act of
receiving the bread and wine. Even here we can lose the

thread if the sermon, for example, is too big or develops a different theme from the whole.

Human contact is vitally important in communication. To have attended a service of worship and not to have made human contact with our brothers and sisters in Christ is a travesty of the corporate nature of worship and communion in particular. The test of our openness to God is always our openness to one another. We specifically include a time of greeting one another in every service – in the Communion this is obviously at the Peace. The whole congregation breaks up in a general hubbub to shake hands or embrace their neighbours, known or unknown. This act affirms our oneness together as forgiven, reconciled children of God and in turn opens us up to him. The quality of singing and participation is enormously improved as a result.

ii) **Variety:** One of the features of a genuine folk expression in worship is variety. If one is to represent the tastes and preferences of the congregation adequately then that implies the use of a wide variety of material so that each grouping has something with which it can identify. Participation is encouraged when there is variety; many more people are actively involved. We have many people of every age participating in worship resource groups from within the congregation. This ranges from the choir to the more informal singing group for family services and the family service orchestra, not to mention the dance, drama and banner groups, the children's workshop who do their own mimes, dances and tableaux, and those who lead services and take prayers.

The actual music reflects this too. Traditional hymns and anthems are juxtaposed with contemporary songs in pop or folk idioms. We monitor the use of this material so that nothing becomes over-used and loses its meaning and freshness as a result. New items are regularly introduced to keep our worship alive to the present activity of the Spirit. Songs tend to come and go in phases. One particular item may be intensely relevant at one period only to fall into disuse later when something else has taken the limelight.

When introducing new music it is important to prepare people. They should be eased into the new with support and encouragement, not just thrown in and left to swim! People often react against the new because no bridges have been built in explaining why such a thing is happening. Ignorance often results in fear and prejudice. Congregational practices are a regular feature of our own services and help people fully to participate in any new music we introduce. Congregational singing can imply the lowest common denominator. With imagination and perseverance this area can be revived for the benefit of all. The alternation of congregation for refrains and choir for more difficult verses can vastly extend the repertoire, and the use of rounds and responsorial or antiphonal devices between a cantor and congregation or between different halves of the congregation can be very stimulating in worship and very satisfying for all. Congregational singing can also be controlled where they are almost too enthusiastic! They do not need to sing everything, all the time. This can severely limit the musical repertoire. Sometimes an anthem or solo item can interpret the theme or mood of a part of the worship more effectively and give everyone a chance to listen and reflect.

Variety is also important in the **structure** of the service. To swop the parts round occasionally avoids predictability and an automatic response to worship. People are easily lulled into mental apathy by familiar word-patterns and actions. They cease to think about what they are doing. A service leader can help in this by a simple re-interpretation or paraphrase of a familiar text.

Careful thought should also be given to the active/passive, sung/spoken, standing/sitting dynamics within the service. For example, if the anthem and readings are put together the congregation remains passive, quiet and sitting for a long time. 'The mind cannot comprehend what the seat cannot endure,' as someone observed! Alternatively, too much standing, singing or other activity can deny people the opportunity for response or reflection. Here, the inclusion of **silence** can be most important in teaching people to listen and absorb God's voice in worship. We can sometimes exhibit a lack of maturity and depth by constantly wanting to move on to the next new or exciting activity without ever giving ourselves the space to assimilate what we have experienced. Silence could be used in personal preparation before worship, after the readings or at the end of a service before the organist launches into a loud and potentially disruptive voluntary. The latter would give people that bit of time to reflect on the impact of the service as a whole before entering the fray once more.

Many services have a 'stop-go' feel to them, like being on a branch line train. We have hardly got going when we stop yet again to do something else! This is the wrong use of variety. It can be very distracting to the building up of concentration and openness to God in worship. A sense of continuity is vital even between very different ingredients. The whole experience of worship should be allowed to flow and evolve naturally, giving time for each aspect to be understood and assimilated before moving on. This is particularly true in the music where a good time of singing and praise can lift a congregation into worship where an isolated song may not.

iii) **Familiarity:** While variety is important in bringing freshness and involvement to worship, familiarity brings security and also freedom. We are creatures of habit. Young children need the security of a familiar routine and it is the same with us. There must be familiar landmarks in worship if people are to be free and confident in their response to God. The new can often create fear and uncertainty. That is why communicating both the object of any innovation, and also one's expectation of others, is so important. As a musical observation, people are much more free to express their worship when they know the songs well. Even books can be inhibiting. Familiar songs learnt by heart can release people to worship – there is nothing in the way. The song has become part of the person.

This can also be true of the liturgy or structure of the service. Constant innovation and re-arrangement of material is of no benefit to anybody. It can be very unsettling. People begin to feel lost and alienated. It is only familiarity which allows change to be made with effect.

One of the disadvantages of the new services which have been introduced over the past few years for example, has been the destruction of a genuine folk tradition of worship owned by generations of people in and outside the Church. It is now no longer possible to recite the Creed or Lord's Prayer whenever called upon without the uncertainty of which version to use. Worship has become much more tied to books which themselves prescribe several alternative ways of doing things. Perhaps as a result we have lost some of the personal, heart-felt response in worship and some of the common ties which have united people all over the land in prayer and song.

In the planning of our own services, we try to maintain some traditional elements, usually including at least two or three well-known hymns. These help visitors and older people especially to identify with services which might otherwise contain much unfamiliar material. The choir sings traditional anthems from time to time and organists and other instrumentalists play items from the classical repertoire as voluntaries or instrumental meditations. The organ maintains its vital accompanying role in worship, but now shares this with guitar, piano and other orchestral instruments.

We are always trying to balance old and new in order to create an expression of worship which is alive to the present but which also nourishes a living tradition from the past. In this way tradition does not need artificial props or justification for its existence but is reinterpreted creatively by each new generation. Familiar and traditional elements in worship give us a sense of continuity with the past. It is important to acknowledge our roots. To be orientated towards a folk expression in worship does not mean amputating our worship from all that is traditional. Michael Marshall in his book *Renewal in Worship* says: 'A healing and living tradition does not need to cut off the hand from the past which can nourish the present. Past and present must together reach out to the future.'

iv) **Spontaneity:** Clifford Longley once wrote in the Times: 'It is almost as if there is a conspiracy between priests, on the one hand, and their congregations on the other, to conduct their worship on the unspoken assumption that God is not listening, that there is no one on the other end of the telephone line, or at most an automatic answering machine.'

Not all worship can be formally structured. If worship is an offering of love there must be room for spontaneity, especially if that love is a growing, changing thing. The Church is the family of God – children sitting at the feet of their Heavenly Father. Worship should therefore be a conversation, a dialogue with two-way communication, not a monologue we conduct with ourselves, crowding God out with our chatter, our music and our ritual.

It is very important in the planning of worship to 'make spaces for God'. For us, this means establishing a basic plan which we then feel free to depart from at any point depending on how the worship develops. We can always return to the established pattern at a later stage. Nearly every service has a more open time of praise structured into it. In the Family Service this is represented by the chorus time where there is a lot of spontaneity. In the Evening Service we include a 15/20 minute time of praise which can include the spontaneous offering of spiritual gifts, singing or testimony.

In Communion we have the time of Administration. This can be a very moving and productive time in the lives of all present. The music and worship penetrate deeply into people's spirits while they receive the sacraments, for prayer and the laying on of hands for healing. People are often moved to tears, either as they sit in the pew or kneel at the rail.

There are further opportunities to be spontaneous elsewhere in the services: the Greeting Time at the beginning is one. Those leading prayers may sometimes intersperse appropriate songs as they go along. The end of the sermon is another point where someone may come forward with a gift of prophecy to offer. On one occasion, at the end of communion, someone in the congregation spontaneously began the hymn 'Thine be the glory.' The celebrant thought this was more suitable than the pre-arranged item. It was obviously a natural expression of worship at the time. We therefore concluded the service with this hymn instead – when we had found the right key on the organ!

There are many occasions when we will change or adapt the elements we have previously planned in order to fit in with the way the Spirit has been leading our worship. We may swop the order of things, adapt prayers or choose other music if it appears that what we had previously arranged is now not so appropriate. The choir may well have rehearsed a particular item extensively for the occasion, but we have had to learn that the

higher priority is to follow the Spirit and enable the
worship to flow freely and deeply through the most
effective means. Nothing is lost; we can always sing our
piece another time!

Another area of spontaneity occurs after the official
close of the service. Generally people are invited to come
forward for particular prayer and ministry if anything in
the service or the sermon has moved or challenged them
or if they have a personal need. Others from the congregation also come forward to pray with them and there
are often little groups of people scattered all over the
church. We feel it important not to leave people hanging
in the air without some personal help if they have been
deeply moved and opened up by the worship.

v) Growth: We are still learning so much how to achieve
a right balance between all the different facets of
worship, particularly between structure and spontaneity. I doubt if we will ever find the perfect solution!
However, there are three principles which we have come
to understand as important in the future development of
our worship life.

The first is EXPECTATION. The verse from James
4:2 – 'You have not because you ask not,' echoes the
tenth Beatitude: 'Blessed is he who expecteth nothing: he
shall not be disappointed'! Although we do expect God to
be working actively in our services, and try to make room
for this to happen, we could still have a much greater
expectation of what God could do in our worship.

We are often too complacent, too self-satisfied as a
congregation. It is so easy for the freedom we have today
to become calcified and rigid and to become the lifeless
tradition of tomorrow. It is impossible to exhaust the
blessings which God wishes to pour out upon his people.
There is always more to be explored.

The second area is in RESPONSIBILITY. Worship is
not a spectator sport which people indulge in from the

safety of the pew! It is not a presentation or a performance from the front. For the Body to function properly it
requires that every member give themselves to worship,
whether down at the front or up in the gallery. It is vitally
important to discover ways to make this possible in
public worship. This is a problem we are grappling with
very much at the moment.

The third area is COURAGE. So many of us have such
fear when we come together. Fear can bind worship
perhaps more than anything else. We know we should
take more risks in exercising our gifts and making
contributions in worship, but fear paralyses us. We need
to learn how to make mistakes and be accepting of one
another so that we grow through them.

Why are we so fearful in worship – especially the more
spontaneous variety? It could be a wrong fear of God: I'm
not worthy; I'm too bad. It could be a wrong fear of
others: What will people think if I raise my hands, or I'm
too emotional, or I sing too enthusiastically? It could be a
fear of what might happen. Perhaps we'll lose control of
the situation and not know what to do. What will happen
if nothing happens??!

If we want to move forward in worship, Expectation,
Responsibility and Courage are areas in which we need
the boldness and confidence of the Holy Spirit to help us
ovecome our human weakness. Only then will we begin
to discover a greater freedom, depth and power in our
worship, whether formal or informal.

TWO: INFORMAL WORSHIP

'Let go and let God' is the text of a poster on my office
wall. It shows a seagull soaring in the bright blue sky. It
sounds simple enough but it takes much faith and courage to abandon the security of familiar and well-worn

structures and cast oneself on God. Somehow it is safer to be organised; much more threatening to be spontaneous. All we have left then is ourselves.

Informal worship throws into relief where we are with God and one another. Its immediacy wakes us up to what is really happening when we worship together. We have to rely much more on the Spirit to guide and direct us. We must be much more personally responsible to hear and sense the voice of the Spirit that he might direct and guide the meeting. Participating in such worship can be a very vulnerable experience, especially for those who lead!

And yet informal worship can be tremendously exciting and uplifting. Let us look first at the underlying dynamic of this worship (something which is sometimes harder to see in formal services); then at some of the particular hallmarks of informal worship; and finally some guidelines on how to lead and enable it.

1) Approaching Worship

'Prepare the way of the Lord,' says Isaiah 40:3–5. In worship we are building a highway, a road made straight, smooth and level so that God may come to us and we may come to him. The valleys of depression must be lifted up. The mountains of fear and doubt brought low. The rough and uneven places of disobedience and wilfulness made smooth. We are preparing a highway in the desert of our own souls so that God's glory may be revealed.

Any kind of corporate worship, whether formal or informal, follows a familiar pattern of preparation and response. People find it almost impossible to worship from cold and need some preparation and acclimatising in order to begin. Music has an important place in this softening process.

Sometimes it is helpful to see things graphically and to use our imagination as we approach and experience worship. Heaven is not literally 'up there', nor does God dwell somewhere just above the altar, but such symbols can help us in our understanding.

Let us imagine the temple of worship described in 1 Pet. 2:5. The stones represent you and me and we are often ill-shaped to fit into such a spiritual building. We come into worship unprepared, probably feeling rushed, preoccupied and all out of sorts with ourselves, other people and with God. These feelings represent a barrier against us experiencing the presence of God or receiving anything from him. It's as if a great door composed of our sin and all which that represents – failure, moods, anger, negative feelings, unworthiness – has shut us out of the temple. We have no expectation and little desire to worship. We are still part of the temple but without our participation it cannot function properly. It will be incomplete.

Those who lead worship are there to enable us to overcome our feelings and find our way into God's presence, a place where we may give and receive in worship. The first thing we must do, whether by ourselves or as a group, is to confess our sin and wipe the dirt from our feet (1 John 1:9). If we have knowingly disobeyed God or been angry with our brother we cannot honestly worship in spirit and in truth. We need to put things right. It may well mean leaving our gift at the altar and seeking out the person we have wronged or who has wronged us before we can go any further. It is that serious!

With God's forgiveness we can take our first step towards worship. Here music can help us tremendously to begin to respond emotionally to the Spirit. Our minds may often assent to the truth but it is our emotions that bind us and keep us from moving towards God or each other. Songs and hymns of praise which concentrate on the objective reality and constancy of God's love can help us overcome our feelings. We might choose a version of Psalm 103 'Bless the Lord O my soul,' or one or two equally positive songs to establish who God is and what our relationship is with him in Christ.

Using music as a stepping stone, we lift the Key of Praise and begin to unlock the door which has kept us outside. As we put aside our negative feelings the

sacrifice of praise brings freedom and release in worship.
When we can begin to praise God for who he is, rather
than how we feel about him or about ourselves, we begin
to respond and build the faith without which it is impossible to please God. The hymns and songs we sing at
the beginning of a meeting are a vehicle of praise. They
can be seen in purely psychological terms: opening us up
emotionally and making us feel secure and at home with
one another. However, there does come a point when
our praise becomes real worship. The Spirit begins to
take over our praises the more we persevere with them.
Perhaps we must first assure God that we are serious
about meeting with him and that we really want to come
to a place of listening and receptiveness.

As we confess our sins we find forgiveness and the
freedom to come in. As we praise with our music the
Holy Spirit lifts it up beyond earthly bounds and brings
us into worship. Through praise and worship a path is
laid for us to walk right into God's presence. It is as if we
arrive on tiptoe, hushed and totally receptive to what
God has to say to us. Sometimes in worship the praise
reaches such a climax that it is no longer necessary to sing
or speak any more. A heavenly peace and calm descends
upon the participants. Psalm 22:3 tells us that God is
enthroned on the praises of his people.

To experience such worship is to feel bathed in the love
of God. We feel utterly at peace, relaxed and open. In
pictorial language, we have entered his throne-room and
are gathered round his feet, waiting for him to speak.
God opens the treasure chest of his gifts and shares them
with us. He may wish to rebuke us for a lack of faith or
obedience, but always he seeks to encourage us and
assure us of his love and care for us when we repent. He
may want to guide us individually or corporately on a
matter where we need to know his will. Some may be sick
and in need of healing in mind or body. Perhaps we will

receive a gift of faith or a word of knowledge which speaks directly into their situation.

Such experiences of worship are impossible to realise if the service or meeting grinds relentlessly on to its conclusion, or the worship leader does not allow people the space and time to respond. This is why silence is so important and why fear and insecurity must not be allowed to fill up every available space with noise. God's voice is a still, small one and is easily drowned out by our own. If we make no space for God and his Spirit we are missing out on the treasures which he has for us. Worship, and praise its herald, are keys to this treasure house.

2) Hallmarks of Informal Worship

One of the most obvious hallmarks of informal worship
in recent years has been the prolific numbers of SIMPLE
WORSHIP SONGS composed for it. These short, simple
'choruses' are designed for the flow and spontaneity of
this kind of worship. They are almost sung meditations
and concentrate on one particular aspect of God's nature
and our response. They are not meant to be theological or
doctrinal statements of belief, but to be the vehicles of the
love and adoration of the heart. People often misunder-
stand their function and dismiss them as too simplistic to
be taken seriously. It is the difference between singing *to*
God and singing *about* him. You don't present the person
you love with a doctrinal thesis on their nature and place
in the universe, you just say 'I love you'!

In informal worship, when people offer prayers or
songs spontaneously to express the love and adoration
they feel towards God at that moment, they need simple,
versatile forms. Prayers read out of books or complicated
six-verse hymns would be quite inappropriate.

Simple choruses, however, have few words, memor-
able tunes and can be easily picked up, even at the first
hearing. This has the powerful effect of gathering everyone up in worship and releasing praise as one people.
The Spirit can use such songs to open us up to God and to
one another. The chorus is not meant to be great music
but in context it can be much more effective than anything else. The fact that it is simple need not make it any
less profound. What statement could be more profound
than 'Jesus is Lord!' Sensitive and interesting harmony
for voices and instruments can further enhance a humble
melody, so long as it does not begin to distract from the
song's meaning or overload it.

Another particular hallmark of informal worship is
SINGING IN THE SPIRIT. This is a spontaneous

expression of joy and praise in the context of a deep experience of worship. People can exercise this gift in private, but in public worship the congregation might begin to improvise melodies round the closing chord of a song, some using the gift of tongues, others using ordinary words or vocalising.

There is nothing manipulative or magical about Singing in the Spirit, nor indeed about speaking in tongues. It can be started or terminated at will and definitely needs the establishment of a key centre for it to work properly. Sometimes the worship leader can announce his intention to begin singing in the Spirit and can start it from 'cold'. Usually however people's shyness and fear needs to be overcome and they must be encouraged.

Singing in the Spirit and tongues are forms of deep communication with God. They bypass the mind with the limitations and inhibitions which it imposes on us while we remain in control of their use. Our spirit is able to sing with the Holy Spirit like the prayer of sighs 'too deep for words' mentioned by St. Paul.

One further hallmark is the exercise of SPIRITUAL GIFTS. Although any gift can be made 'spiritual' if exercised in the right way, I am talking here more about those mentioned by St. Paul in 1 Cor. 12:8–10.

Renewal has brought these particular gifts into focus in the last few years. Until recently, many people had thought they were given only for the establishment of the Early Church and were not to be expected today. In informal worship however, one is very likely to come across a gift of prophecy, a word of knowledge, the gift of tongues or healing. It is important for us to be prepared and to know how to make a response.

The right use of spiritual gifts of whatever kind depends on our attitude. Even the most spiritual sounding gifts like healing or prophecy can be used in a wrong and 'fleshly' way. The crucial test is given by St. Paul in 1 Cor. 12:3. The gift must exalt Jesus as Lord, the constant ministry of the Holy Spirit. Gifts must also build up the Body. Verse 7: 'To each is given the manifestation of the Spirit for the common good.' One good test of attitude is whether we regard a gift as 'my' gift or 'God's' gift?

One of the dangers in the use of gifts is to slip into feelings of jealousy or pride and to begin to compare gifts on an ascending scale. Paul describes this in terms of people with an *inferiority complex* (v. 15), or a *superiority complex* (v. 21). Both attitudes are wrong. All gifts are for service and a gift does not bestow special worth or importance on its possessor. As in everything else, *love* is the acid test (ch. 13). The Holy Spirit will witness personally to us whether a gift is excercised in love. We will sense an uneasiness within or an abrasiveness in the way it is used if this is not so. We should trust such feelings.

In informal worship, the leader (be it minister or musician) must provide a covering for these gifts and encourage the congregation to weigh carefully what has been said. This is to discern whether or not it is God speaking or just someone's 'nice thoughts'.

The *gift of prophecy* is the speaking out of God's mind. A person has an increasing conviction that God is wanting to say something to the assembly. It may be something they have carried with them for a number of days. God's desire is always to build up and encourage his people and this will be reflected in what is said. If the prophecy contains a rebuke it will always be set in the context of love and will give people the opportunity to respond and change. Condemnatory prophecy and prophecy which gives too specific directions should be treated with caution.

The human influence on any spiritual gift is unavoidable, hence the vital importance of 'weighing' gifts and opening them up for scrutiny and discussion. Each individual must make up his own mind and be encouraged to discern what God may be saying to him personally. A person who is not open to having his gift weighed by his brothers and sisters, or who places too much emphasis on 'thus saith the Lord,' almost invalidates it. The ultimate test of all spiritual gifts is in their effectiveness and degree of response: 'By their fruits ye shall know them'!

The *Word of Knowledge* is given out by a person who receives an impression that God wishes to heal or deal with a specific illness or problem of an unknown person in the assembly. The individual with the gift has no previous knowledge nor indeed could have had. Speaking it out encourages faith and the ability in the individual concerned to receive what God wants to do.

Tongues are often given out and an interpretation like a prophecy is given by the same person or another within the group. The tongues wake people up to the supernatural (God is really there!) and prepare people to receive what God wants to say. At other times they can be pure praise.

The *ministry of healing* is increasing in importance these days. The atmosphere of informal worship is extremely helpful in preparing and opening people to the influence of the Holy Spirit. Even in the context of a formal service the time of ministry could be helpfully accompanied by gentle, sensitive songs of worship. The gift of healing should always bring glory to Jesus Christ, it should issue in worship as a test of its authenticity.

It is so important in times of worship to allow spaces where people can respond, particularly when a climax of praise is reached. This is equally true for those with gifts. Someone may need to be quiet in order to hear the Lord speaking to them, or to pluck up courage to give out a word of prophecy, of knowledge or a tongue. Just recently, in our preparation before services, we have begun to pray quite specifically for such gifts to be manifested and to know what God wants to do among us.

3) Leading Informal Worship

The Key of Praise

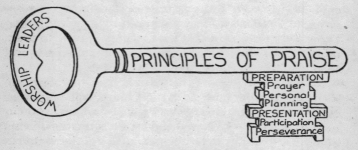

Leading worship of whatever kind is an art, but particularly in informal or spontaneous worship. The leader must be doubly prepared for the unexpected and able to be discerning, adaptable and flexible in making a response. The event is unfolding moment by moment and the leader has the responsibility to oversee its progress and influence it by his decisions. This Key of Praise, which I have chosen to call it, must be manipulated with skill if it is to unlock our worship and lead us into God's presence. As praise is very often a musical activity, the following advice has a musical slant. Leading praise and worship is not the exclusive domain of the musician however and the most effective leadership will be a shared one between all the parties involved.

The first principle in this key is PREPARATION. Spontaneity, if is to succeed, requires great preparation. The stand-up comic practises the timing and delivery of his jokes for hours on end; the jazz saxophonist puts in a lot of practice on his instrument in order to be able to play his breaks so fluently. To improvise at all the musician or dancer must have a vocabulary of experience to draw on in order to interpret the present.

Leading worship is a priestly role. The Levites in the Temple prepared themselves carefully for the task. They cleansed and purified themselves, donned special robes and offered appropriate sacrifices. They acted as ushers, enabling people to come before God in worship. We too have the same task and, like servants of a great king must know him, have access to him and know how to bring others to him. We need to know what we are doing and this skilled task requires training and practice.

How can we prepare? Here, individual and corporate PRAYER is important, asking that God will cleanse us and make us ready to serve him in this way. We need our minds and spirits to be aware and sensitive to the moving of his Spirit. We pray that he will give us expectation in our worship and enable us to build faith for what God wants to do.

What we are doing must of course be PERSONAL to each one of us. We are not just singing a string of songs or spouting words automatically. We should 'embody' what we are singing or speaking about, individually and as a group. We lead by example more than by our words. If we are singing 'the joy of the Lord is my strength,' while looking thoroughly miserable, or 'take my life and let it be,' while gazing around absentmindedly, it is unlikely that people will take the message of the song seriously. You may have heard of the Duke of Plaza Toro in Gilbert and Sullivan's comic opera *The Gondoliers*. He fully expressed the essence of bad leadership:

> In enterprise of martial kind
> Where there was any fighting,
> He led his regiment from behind,
> He found it less exciting.

PLANNING is the next part of our preparation. We are to be 'equipped, ready for every good work'. We should not be afraid of planning; 'administration' is a spiritual gift (1 Cor. 12:28). Things don't usually 'just happen' – God uses *people* to accomplish his will. 'Oh', we say, 'it will be all right on the night'. Unfortunately it very often isn't and we end up confusing and embarrassing people instead!

There is a very practical side to leading worship, especially at the beginning. Some people think that an off-the-cuff sing-song of random songs will somehow produce a spirit of worship. Choices are requested from the floor, sometimes totally inappropriate to the occasion, or else catching the musicians without the music or the necessary expertise. Instead, we need to do some homework first and not expect the Holy Spirit to pick up the pieces of our laziness. We could:

○ Think of which songs sum up what God is saying and doing in the church at the moment, and which fit with the theme of the meeting.

○ Think which selection of songs would fit together to provide a natural sequence of praise and worship in terms of mood, theme, or key. We need a flow and continuity to build worship. If two adjacent songs have extreme key-changes this can jar the nerves and cause a hiatus while the guitarist adjusts his *capo*.

○ Choose a lively, familiar song to begin with which draws people together. Then consolidate with another which begins to open people up in praise. Let them lead naturally into shorter, more sensitive, personal choruses that could also become spontaneous from the congregation. They could all be in the same or related keys so as not to interrupt the flow. These should encourage a quiet and receptive waiting upon God.

○ Have a plan A. It's easy to get stuck if we haven't thought things through. On the spur of the moment we may have a blank and not be able to think of anything appropriate. We may lose our nerve and end up with a fumbling, embarrassing hiccup in the worship which destroys the atmosphere. If we assume things will just happen we may lose the confidence of the congregation. They will stop trusting us and we will not be able to continue to lead them. Instead, have a few songs up your sleeve.

Having prepared ourselves to lead worship we should now look at our PRESENTATION. The way we conduct and present ourselves is vitally important in building people's confidence in our ability to lead them.

Do we come up to the front in a chaotic ragged manner, having to go back again because we have forgotten something? Perhaps we communicate a lack of care and preparation by a slovenly and casual entrance. Have we thought about where we are going to sit or stand, or do we spend the first few minutes jostling each other to get into position or just amass in an untidy lump?

How we stand is also important. We want to encourage people by inviting them to join with us in worship. Use eyes and eyebrows to interpret the words and a body position which is open and welcoming, not stiff and backing away as if we wanted to leave on the earliest possible train! Be real and natural. Share the joy of the Lord in faces as well as voices. This is all part of embodying praise.

We need to relate well together – to feel secure and confident with each other and whoever is leading at the time. This person should get our undivided attention, there should be no back-chat or by-play that so often betrays nerves or insecurity. In-jokes should be avoided and the classic turn-off of all amateur performers: 'I hope you'll excuse our lack of rehearsal / voices / tuning of the guitar' etc., etc.! We should know the material and trust the accompaniment because it has been well prepared. All small or insignificant details are worthy of attention.

For example, can we all see each other so that we can encourage one another with eye-contact as we go along? Who is introducing what? Have people thought through their verbal introductions to avoid waffle? Songs sometimes need a few words of introduction to bring out the theme or to help people to sing them with meaning, but this should not be allowed to develop into a mini sermon!

Musical introductions also need care to ensure that everyone knows exactly where to come in. So often the instrumentalist launches into a song in completely the wrong rhythm – three-time when it should be four, or in the wrong key – so high that the song experiences an untimely death in laughter and confusion!

Have we prepared the bogey of all modern performers – the P.A.!? Does the operator know his cues or how to balance the musical sound? Remember you are entrusting the final results of all your careful efforts to him! Do you yourselves know how to use the microphones correctly? Are they adjusted to the right height? I heard of one bishop who got up into the pulpit to preach and found the microphone wasn't working. 'There's something wrong with the microphone,' he said. The congregation, seeing his lips move but not hearing what he said, dutifully responded, 'And also with you.'

Endings also need to be planned. How does the song end and who is going to introduce the next item? Have they gone to sleep? Maybe they are in the wrong place and waste valuable seconds getting to the mike. Even the way the group finishes or makes its exit is important so that the atmosphere of worship is not destroyed.

To lead worship effectively we must keep alert and know what song is coming up. If there are hiccups, carry on regardless and don't make a big thing of mistakes –

just ignore them. Spontaneity in worship can be aided by having an index in the song-book! Also, prepare people for uncertainty. Tell them if it is an open time of worship and even how long it is likely to last. Give them some idea of what this time will involve if they are new to the experience.

Other practical areas of presentation include general tidiness of books and papers – get away from them completely if you can. This makes an incredible difference to the feeling of freedom and versatility. Even a professional choir communicates much better without the barrier of printed music.

Think about dress too. Clashing colours can be very distracting and pink, spikey hair off-putting to older members! Too much matching and toning of clothes and colours can be rather 'twee'.

The most important thing about leading worship is to encourage PARTICIPATION. It is not a performance and not an opportunity to do all your favourite songs and miss out all the ones you don't like! We must be sensitive to the mood of the meeting and flow with it as the Spirit leads. We are to help people respond to God through our use of music, expecting the Spirit to show us songs to initiate that will help them most. We must encourage Body participation, making it easy for people to respond with songs, testimony or spiritual gifts. We should not be afraid to take a lead while at the same time making room for others. If someone else starts a song, support them by helping everyone else to join in. We may need to change the key or the speed if necessary at a natural break. If it is too high or too low decide as soon as possible then change it confidently, with no hesitation.

If someone else has the ball of leadership, allow them the responsibility to take over at that time. Don't cut across them with your own ideas which you may feel are better, or be over-controlling. We must be careful not to manipulate the direction in which we think things should be going. If however, we are getting sidetracked, or losing our way, we should gently guide things back. If a person starts an inappropriate song or shares a prophecy that doesn't seem right, we must have the courage to correct or gently disagree. The congregation will be relying on us to take the responsibility for leadership which they have invested in us.

The last section in the Key of Praise is PERSEVERANCE. We must persevere in praise and worship right into God's presence. So often we get stuck, hovering on the doorstep. We lose our nerve or our concentration. We are afraid of losing control – what might happen?? Instead, we should sustain our praise as long as it is necessary for the Holy Spirit to move us into worship and create the flow and immediacy which is the mark of his presence. We will hardly ever go on too long. Usually things are just beginning to take off when we curtail events and move on to the next part of the service. Perhaps we should take a leaf out of some African churches' worship where the singing goes on for hours, even before the actual service begins, and some songs are repeated twenty or thirty times! If we are getting bored in worship, stop singing the same old songs and introduce some new ones.

Worship can be like flying a kite. Some days we can spend all the time running backwards and forwards in a frantic effort to get the thing off the ground. While we are running the kite lifts a little up into the air, but as soon as we stop, it sinks down to the ground again. We expend vast amounts of energy singing hymns and planning liturgies all to no avail. We certainly need the human effort to get things off the ground and into the air-currents but ultimately we need the wind of the Spirit to fly successfully. Then there is no effort involved. We have done our part in making the kite and launching it into the air, but it is the Holy Spirit who must lift us up into the thermals of God's activity. All these things are the preparation for 'lift-off'!

4

THE PLACE OF MUSIC

There was once a large poster on a church notice board which asked: 'Do you want to know what hell is like?'

Underneath was pinned a smaller notice: 'Remember Choir Practice, every Friday, 7.30 p.m.!'

Many churches today are experiencing tensions in their music. There is suspicion and misunderstanding between organists and vicars, choirs and congregations – even resulting in strikes! One headline I saw recently said: 'Choir walks out on note of discord.' The vicar was accused by the organist of wanting to introduce 'a lot of "Clap hands here comes Charlie" services', addressing God as 'You', and having 'little groups of people with guitars doing their nasty, folky stuff'. 'All quite ghastly,' he said!

Many issues are at stake: the very role of the choir and organist, traditional versus new music, new forms of service, robes, male versus mixed choirs etc. The list is endless. It seems ironic that a body like the choir, called together to lead and inspire worship should often be such a hotbed of discontent – almost as if, had the devil wished to disrupt the worship of God more, he could not have chosen a better vehicle! As a Mr. Sargeant of Clifton Chapel once remarked: 'God made the church, the devil made the choir!'

What are we to make of it all? How has it come about that the area of music in worship, far from being full of peace and harmony, is so full of disharmony? Perhaps it comes down to a misunderstanding of what music in worship is all about. We will look first at the place of music in worship, then its place in the witness and mission of the Church.

ONE: MUSIC IN WORSHIP

1) The Gift of God

Music is a gift of God. In the dictionary it is defined as 'the art of combining sounds with a view to beauty of form and expression of emotion.' Music is given as a thing of beauty to be delighted in. As such it is a universal gift, not just for the enjoyment of God's people, but for all mankind. There is no such thing as 'Christian' music, any more than there are 'Christian' roses. Music in itself is neutral, although the associations brought to it by words or performers appear to influence it one way or another. The melodies, chords and rhythms in themselves have no inherent moral value, even though our different cultural backgrounds would persuade us otherwise.

In medieval times the interval of the augmented fourth or 'Tritone' was symbolic of the devil and was to be avoided at all costs. We have no qualms about using it today. To our Western ears, some oriental music sounds very strange but is obviously perfectly acceptable in the East. Even the physical laws of music which affect the stability or instability of intervals (like the perfect fifth or the major second) can affect different racial or cultural groups in different ways.

There has been a lot of debate recently about the acceptability of Rock music in Christian worship. Some view it as anathema, tainted by the evils of African spiritism and black magic. They see it as manipulative and as appealing to the darker impulses of human nature. Sometimes the heavy beat and dubious lyrics would seem to support this. But many Christian performers involved in the pop music scene have embraced Rock music and used it for communicating the Gospel. Their view is the one first expressed by Roland Hill: 'Why should the devil have all the good music?' They believe in redeeming music as a gift to be used for the glory of God, in all its range and variety. To begin to make moral judgments as to the worth of different styles of music and the moral calibre of composers and performers really does become a nonsense. So many of the great classical composers could hardly be considered committed Christians, and yet they produced masterpieces which reveal something of the meaning and glory of life. Their works are windows on eternity through which we may well glimpse God. I love the music of Delius and the way in which it captures the spirit and beauty of nature and the exhilaration of being alive; and yet Delius had no belief in God and indulged in profligacy during his life, ultimately dying of syphilis.

Our God is too small if he is only able to speak through one kind of art form stamped with the orthodox seal of approval. The whole world and everything in it was created by God. Every human being reflects something of the image of his creator whether he is regenerate or not. Sometimes we may find the Spirit of God is working more outside Christian circles than within! We limit the love of God and fail to realise that God is involved with every human being in every place. I remember a one-time leader of the Jesus People in California saying how impressed he was at the radicalism and sheer originality of new British pop music. The breaking-out of tradition, the questioning and searching for truth and reality, he viewed as signs of the Holy Spirit's activity in the nation. The Spirit was creating a vacuum, a hunger for spiritual values and meaning for life which only God could fill. Certainly the number of Christian artists in the pop scene and the numbers of young people turning to Christ is no small phenomenon today. There is an openness to God often lacking in the materialistic well-being of the older generation.

2) The Overflow of Life

We can therefore redeem and bring into worship every kind of musical expression if it is truly part of us and witnesses to the power of God at work in our lives from day to day. It becomes the overflow of hearts and lives given to God.

St. Augustine wrote: 'Singing comes from joy, but if we observe more carefully, we see that it comes from love, we sing about what we love.'

Music provides a release, giving voice to pent-up feelings and expressing joy, sadness, aspiration and the whole gamut of human experience, much of which cannot be expressed in words. But above all, for the Christian, it expresses love. If love is the greatest and highest ideal in life, then music, if it is to achieve a spiritual end, must flow from love, the love of God and the love of fellow human beings.

Paul Tortelier, speaking recently of his retirement from international cello playing, said that what he was looking forward to most in retirement, was being able to spend more time at home with his wife. His period away from home had been a difficult sacrifice to make in his professional career. Life, he said, was more about love between people than anything else, and not even the love of music should come before that.

The style of music we use in worship and the quality of the resources we have to perform it are, in the end, unimportant compared with the quality of our love and commitment to one another and our life in God. Many people try to revamp their music and services to make them more attractive, more exciting, more contemporary. These are temporary cures. If we want our music and worship to have depth, reality and integrity, we need to look at the heart of what we are doing. We need to examine our individual experience of God and the corporate life we have with each other. At York, the music and worship have grown hand in hand with the pains and joys of relating together. There are no short-cuts!

3) Bringing the Best

There are a number of things in churches which people hold very dear and defend most strongly if threatened with change. One is the language of worship (1662 and all that), another is the ritual (or lack of it), and a third is the music. The vicar may deny the basic tenets of the faith from the pulpit, or run off with the church-warden's wife, the numbers of the congregation may be dropping to zero and the level of giving may be appalling, but they are all as nothing compared with altering a word in the communion service or performing a song with guitars!

Why? Because things like music are felt to be owned by everyone. Not everybody can preach or lead prayers but everyone can sing. It is therefore considered their right to determine the shape of their music; they know best. This is probably true, but what is 'best'?

Some may consider classical music to be the best medium for the worship of God. It has stood the test of time and therefore proved its worth. For them the modern phenomenon of 'throw-away' music seems a dreadfully unworthy approach in worship. But traditional music is often better quality simply because all the rest has been politely disposed of by succeeding generations! Few of the great composers ever expected their works to last beyond their own life-time. Preservation is a relatively modern preoccupation!

For others the guitar must be in evidence to give worship any spiritual validity. Traditional music is 'out'. 'Sing a *new* song' the Bible says. Worship must be an immediate 'While-U-Wait' experience!

People have very different ideas of what is 'best'. It all depends on upbringing, education and individual taste. Dean William Inge made a wise comment when he wrote: 'There are two kinds of fools: one says, "This is old, therefore it is good," the other says, "This is new, therefore it is better."'

To consider what is the best music we can use for worship we must think about the circumstances. What is the setting – cathedral or country chapel – what is the age and size of the congregation, what is their social background – working or middle class, intellectual, etc., etc. – What is the strength and quality of the musical resources?

Music needs to scratch where the congregation itches! It has to be functional and relevant to their needs. The best music for worship will be that which sums up the heart of the people and with which they can identify most. Michael Baughen, Bishop of Chester, once likened music in worship to a tin-opener. What is the best tin-opener you could buy – a gold-plated one? No, one that opens tins! The gold-plated one would look very beautiful, you could put it in a case and admire it. But you need one made of ordinary steel with a sharp point to get at the nourishing contents inside. When you have opened it, you don't sit and wonder at the beauty of the tin-opener, your focus of attention is now on the contents. It may be far-fetched to imagine worship as the opening up of so many baked beans in a tin, but it makes the point!

4) The Servant of Worship

Our recent experience in Western music of the Great Composer acting like a high priest of his art has possibly coloured our approach to music and its function in worship. We look for great art to fulfil our needs in worship thinking that somehow the presence of God will be found here rather than in simpler, humbler forms. We often give music too great a significance and end up glorifying the gift rather than using it as a pointer towards God.

Instead, music is to be the servant of worship, nothing special in itself, but a vehicle which carries us from A to B. It may be grand and luxurious like a Rolls Royce, or humble like a bicycle. The important thing is that we reach our destination where we get out and enjoy the new surroundings. If, through music, we are carried into the presence of God and are able freely to express our worship, then it has fulfilled its function admirably.

In worship, music has a secondary role and this can sometimes be hard to accept if you are a musician and a particular piece means a lot to you. Our music is there to serve a higher aim, no matter how great a piece of art it is, or how excellently it is performed. Sometimes, perhaps often, it will be the humble hymn or chorus which will best sum up people's worship. The musician may prefer an anthem but he must learn to be humble enough in his position to put aside his own preference.

If music is the servant of worship, the musician is servant of the people. Unfortunately, many owe their allegiance more to church music, the choir or the organ than to the Lord and his people. They are not really in touch with the pulse or heart-beat of worship and are not really integrated into the life of the church. In the Bible the servant performed the menial, mundane chores like washing feet or preparing food. These were important tasks but were directed solely towards the master. We as musicians offer the music as a service to the congregation. If, like the clergy, we wear robes, they are only the livery indicating that we are there to serve, not something that raises our status and makes us special or separate from everyone else.

The church musician is first and foremost a member of the Body of Christ. In a way his gift, though significant, is incidental and is not the chief reason for his being a member of the church. Unless he has this commitment and is willing to submit his musical gift to the vision of the church, he will be worse than useless in performing music as a ministry to the people.

To use music as a spiritual gift requires great care and sensitivity. Its position is very important in the experience of worship but the element of performance makes it open to abuse. All gifts belong to God. If we use them in the wrong way, say for personal aggrandisement, the Spirit very quietly leaves and our gift soon becomes fruitless. Lionel Dakers sums it up:

> A person sensitive in both spiritual and musical spheres can sense, almost immediately, whether a particular performance of a liturgical work, is regarded by the performers as 'pure' music or prayer . . . Even in parish churches that have struggled to keep alive a local church music tradition (and in this age the struggle is an uphill one) it is the exception rather than the rule to find that the music is being prayed rather than merely 'performed'.

5) Music as Ministry

How can we learn to use our music as a ministry? Music has such special significance in the leading of praise and worship that it must first of all be used with great *integrity*.

Jesus, in John 4:24, told us to worship the Father 'in spirit and truth', while the prophet Amos warns of the dangers of singing praises to God when we are not living out our faith: 'Stop your noisy songs, I do not want to listen to your harps. Instead, let justice flow down like a stream and righteousness like a river that never goes dry' (Amos 5:23).

Our music should have integrity, but it should also have *sensitivity*: 'Singing to a person who is depressed is like taking off his clothes on a cold day!' (Proverbs 25:20 GNB). When music loses sensitivity to the Holy Spirit it is no longer a ministry. It has become an end in itself, either in satisfying our own emotions or as a performance. The musician must not only be sensitive to the voice of the Spirit, but also be aware of the need and desire of the people. How often the music we use in worship and the way we present it prove entirely inappropriate. We choose obscure or complicated music which only a small musical elite can appreciate. We sing bouncy, extrovert choruses when we should be thoughtful, even silent. We stuff hymns and anthems into the service like 'musical Polyfilla', as Michael Marshall terms it, with little regard for the theme or mood of the event.

Such practices destroy any sense of ministry. Learning to gauge the mood and direction of worship and to tune into the flow of the Spirit is a sign of maturity in worship leadership and takes time to learn. The musician's role is to draw people into a place of openness and attentiveness to God. His ministry has special importance in the life of the church, just as it did in the Temple, helping to set the spiritual tone and receptiveness of the congregation as it grows in the life of the Spirit.

Through being sensitive to the mood and feelings of those we are leading we can make our music a source of great *encouragement*. It can fix our eyes on the God 'whose steadfast love never ceases'. In the same way that David's music soothed the troubled Saul, music can often bring a deep healing and refreshment. It can penetrate our thoughts and emotions in a way that words cannot. Someone once mentioned how my oboe playing in worship had helped restore them at a time when they felt bruised and discouraged.

When music draws us into worship, it can make us more aware of God and help us to hear his voice. At a diocesan synod recently, the members found a short music practice a useful way of focusing and drawing them together before the process of decision-making began!

Music in worship can facilitate a greater responsiveness to the Holy Spirit. In the Old Testament there are two examples which illustrate the use of music in enabling the prophetic gift. In 2 Kings 3:15, Elisha summons a minstrel in order to prophesy to the King of Israel: 'And when the musician played, the power of the Lord came upon him. And he said "Thus says the Lord . . ."'

Earlier, in 1 Sam. 10:5, a band of prophets is described coming down the mountain singing, playing instruments and prophesying with great abandon. (Note that even at this time the two streams of folk and liturgical music existed side by side.) We may also experience something similar today. In our own congregation those who are believed to have the gift of prophecy say how much easier it is to hear what God wants to say to his people after a time of praise and worship.

Music also has an important ministry in the context of teaching. In Colossians 3 the teaching is set among the singing of psalms, hymns and spiritual songs. The power of setting doctrine or important spiritual truths to music in order to teach them, has long been proven. One disgruntled Catholic in Luther's time complained bitterly that through his popular hymns 'The whole people is learning itself into this Lutheran doctrine.'

Setting the Scriptures to music helps us to remember its truths and establish them in our hearts. We can learn verses easily when they are presented in the form of a song: the rhythm and melody of the music helps to fasten them in our minds. Jesus himself used this principle in his teaching. In the original Aramaic, the parables have a particular rhythmic form which helped ordinary people remember them. Moses also knew how useful music could be in communicating God's law. Before he died, he left a song extolling the name of the Lord, his loving care for his people, his mercy and righteousness, sharply contrasted against their ingratitude and faithlessness. Before he gave it, he said, 'Write this song and . . . put it in their mouths' (Deut. 31:19 RSV). And afterwards he enjoined them to 'make sure you obey all these commands that I have given you today. Repeat them to your children so that they may faithfully obey all God's teachings' (Deut. 32:46 GNB).

In the twentieth century the power of songs to communicate creed or life-style is particularly evident. The advertising jingle indelibly etches its message on our minds, ruining the most sublime musical masterpiece by associating it forever with brown bread or a certain brand of cigar! Such is music's power to convey a worldly message. We can learn to use it to convey the greatest message of all time, that 'God so loved the world . . .' and to put that message on our lips and in our hearts.

6) Brokenness

Human energy and talent ultimately accomplish nothing for the Kingdom of God unless they have come through the cross of Christ. Real ministry, that is communicating the life of God in some way to another person, comes through brokenness. It was the way of the cross which

Jesus took in order to give life to others, and it must be our way too.

We have many gifts: music, leadership, speaking, helping etc.; but the only way to release the aroma of Christ is to allow God to break us open. God must break our pride and our reliance on position or gifts for our self-respect. He must also break us open to one another to create a real unity of spirit where we are all equal before him in our weakness. The alabaster jar of precious ointment had to be broken open before the woman could anoint Jesus, but when it had been, the aroma filled the house.

I experienced something of this in my own life when I gave up my music at the end of university with the intention of entering the ordained ministry. This did not work out as I expected. I was refused and after a time of doubt and uncertainty, found myself returning to York to play the organ at St. Cuthbert's.

I had offered my life and my gifts to God expecting him to lead me in one direction and ended up with the best of both worlds, serving him and using my music! But this was now held in more open palms and the experience of releasing my gift to God made me more malleable and adaptable in the job he gave me to do. I no longer had such heavy personal investment and ambition in my music, an element which tends to mar many gifts. When as an organist I felt really threatened by the introduction of guitars, my trust in God and his people enabled me to face my reactions and press through them into a place of freedom. Without an element of brokenness I might easily have clutched tightly on to my position and strangled the life of the Spirit in myself and others in the process.

TWO: MUSIC AND MISSION

'Worship in ruins!' proclaimed a front page headline in the *Church Times*, as if sounding the death-knell for many a parish: 'Easingwold Town Band will take part in an open-air service in the ruins of Byland Abbey.'

What is the quality of our worship today? Is it dying on its feet? Worship is one of the Cinderellas of church life. A. W. Tozer once called it 'the missing jewel of the Evangelical Church,' but this could well apply in many other traditions.

In general, people have not grasped the significance of worship in church life and the implications a renewed and vibrant worship life might have. Not only would it lead to a greater openness of individuals and fellowships to the activity of the Spirit but it would also vastly increase the influence and authority of the church's message in the surrounding community.

Worship has been called the Church's shop window. Through worship we witness to the world of the reality of God among us (or the opposite of course). If music is the main vehicle for worship we can see how important the style and spiritual quality of our music is. How does the pattern and style of our worship bear on our witness in the local community? What role has music to play in this as a vital, determining force? What are our attitudes as musicians, clergy or congregations towards the relevance to contemporary society of the music we employ in worship? How flexible are we to change and adapt? Let us examine some of these important questions.

1) Praise Communicates

Worship is a powerful evangelistic agent. On the Day of Pentecost the Holy Spirit's dramatic intervention into the lives of the first disciples attracted an enormous crowd.

People heard the glory of God extolled in their own languages. Peter preached his famous sermon explaining what was happening and how others might also share in the experience. Three thousand people were brought into the Church in one day. Later, in Acts 2:43–47 the common life of praise and sharing among the disciples witnessed powerfully to the community around them and 'the Lord added to their number day by day those who are being saved.'

There is a close link between the praise of God and powerful evangelism. When worship is marked by the freshness and freedom of the Holy Spirit, people are attracted and want to know what's going on. As someone put it: 'A praising community preaches to answer questions raised by its praise.' Our trouble is usually that we are preaching, but no one is asking any questions! Most of the time we are not even speaking to people in a language they can understand. The Scriptures specifically say that each one 'heard them speaking in his own language'. This amazed them and increased enormously the impact of the event. People are similarly amazed today when they hear us in the Church speaking to them in ways that they can understand. The power of the Gospel to change and challenge lives has in no way been diminished. But we can conceal the truth by the traditions and trappings we employ. Our music does the same. Why are our churches failing to attract the large numbers of people seen by the Early Church? The answer is complex, but here are two possible reasons:

Firstly, few churches today experience a vibrant, corporate life in which the Spirit of God is actively present. Worship, rather than being the jewel in the crown of our activity, often seems boring and unattractive. The lives of Christians are not noticeably different from their counterparts in the world. The Church is a spiritual country-club.

When the Holy Spirit begins to move in a congregation he brings new wine. This needs new wineskins. Old ones – traditional structures and old ways of doing things – are simply inadequate to contain it. They crack and burst under the strain. No wonder the process is often traumatic and many prefer to remain safe and unruffled where they are. There should be something different about our worship when it has been touched afresh by the Spirit. In it the outsider should sense a spring-like quality, a freshness brought by the presence of God.

Secondly, the Church has lost touch with contemporary society. The cultural life of young people changes at least once every five years. The Church's rate of change is desperately slow. David Winter has put it so: 'In the institutional, moribund, introverted ranks of our Christian churches, we have a private dialogue with ourselves while man plunges suicidally on into absurdity and despair.'

People are crying out for meaning and purpose in life but they dismiss the Church and its message as utterly irrelevant. We have lost communication. This equally applies to our music and makes it even more significant when one realises that today's culture among young people, and increasingly among older people too, revolves chiefly around their music. The type of music we use as Christians says so much about ourselves and the nature of our God.

2) 'The Medium is the Message'

What then is our music and worship communicating? It may be very different from what we think. For example, if in public worship our music never ventures beyond the 1900s what impression are we giving? Surely that our God is the God of yesterday. Similarly, if we confine our music to serious, 'highbrow' styles we will unconsciously suggest that God belongs only to middle class intellectuals and not to simpler people. This could be extended to styles of architecture, vestments, graphic design etc., etc. I remember taking part in an anglo-catholic mass in one parish church. The Bishop was present and we had all the trappings. I have a great respect for the high-church tradition but on this occasion I could not help noticing a number of things: the sentimental mural of Christ above the altar with its peeling paintwork; the faded, threadbare vestments with their dull, dreary designs; the deadly boring hymns; and the coughing and spluttering of the reader as he attempted the Gospel of the Day amid clouds of suffocating incense. The participants were sincere and devoted Christians but the media they were using to express their worship was so out of date. It was a strange anachronism.

To a lesser degree similar things are taking place in our worship every Sunday throughout the land. How can the Gospel be seen to be relevant to a modern world when almost everything in the church is the product of a past era? The medium has become a negative message denying the true message of the Gospel. Tradition is important in maintaining balance and a sense of perspective but not at the expense of relevance and life itself. So we must be ruthless in our appraisal of what we are doing and how we are communicating our message. Then we can begin to consider realistically how much of our present forms of worship and witness we can *afford* to keep.

As worship leaders in the church, musicians must ask themselves serious questions about the musical styles they do, or do not permit. What are their reasons behind employing certain kinds of music and modes of performance? They may find themselves not only inhibiting the free expression of the congregation's worship, but also hindering the way the reality of Christ is communicated to the world outside. How much do we care about the many people who have great difficulty in responding to the present musical framework of our services?

Canon Alan Warren wrote in the *Church Times*: 'Must we inevitably demand of all believers, not only commitment to Jesus Christ, but also commitment to *Hymns Ancient and Modern* (or should it be *Ancient and Victorian*?), commitment to the apparently irreplaceable sound of the pipe organ, or even the specialised musical ethos of choral evensong?'

Another parody, this time of a nursery rhyme, put it:

> Rector, rector, choir director,
>   How is your church today?
> With canticles and chiming bells,
>   While most folk stay away!

3) 'Something old, something new'

What can be done? What style of music should be encouraged – Pop, 'Heavy Metal', 'Funk', or 'The Sound of Kings'? As usual for most of us the answer probably lies in compromise. Certainly it lies in a realistic assessment of the local church, its membership and its area of witness.

In a splintered society worship needs to be a wholesome, unifying act. It should blend the old and the new, the formal and the spontaneous, just as a congregation should include people of every age, culture, class and education. Some say styles of worship must be relevant above all else. Others, that the pursuit of beauty and perfection in worship is all-important. There is always a temptation, particularly in music, to polarise and choose one way to the exclusion of all others.

Compromise is an untidy, messy business! Yet to

choose one way to the exclusion of the other is escaping from the ministry of reconciliation which we have in Christ. We are to reconcile different and sometimes contradictory poles of opinion and to exhibit the love of Christ which transcends barriers of taste, background or prejudice. If worship is the Church's shop window, it must display a good selection of fruits, particularly love and acceptance.

Church musicians need to be open to every style of music so that they may apply their discernment right across the board. The renewal movement has given many good things to the Church, but its music has often been very poor in quality. This is not surprising when many musicians have remained superior and aloof! Where are the musicians, broad-minded and well-educated enough to discern the quality of the new popular music? Most are out of touch and possibly quite inept at passing judgment. To serve our congregations we must put aside patronising attitudes or an unwillingness to familiarise ourselves with popular styles and idioms. I may not personally enjoy the hymns of Moody and Sankey or their modern equivalents but they are obviously meaningful and have a special appeal to many people.

It is easy to condemn the traditionalist and there is just as much arrogance and narrow-mindedness shown by those who reject out of hand all that is old or traditional. Many people, at the mention of classical music, immediately close their ears and their minds. They make no attempt to understand or appreciate it. To be seen to indulge in it would be to let the side down. Classical music is an acquired taste. It needs a certain amount of mental effort and background knowledge to appreciate it. It is not as immediate as 'pop' music, but in the end it can pay greater dividends.

A mature and reasonable compromise in the music we

use for worship enables us to move forward together. Continuing to be starkly divided between classical and popular approaches only leaves both the poorer. They need each other: as Jesus said: 'Every scribe who has been trained for the kingdom of heaven is like a house-holder who brings out of his treasure something old and something new' (Matt. 13:52).

4) Bringing All

In worship we need the traditional elements to provide stability and continuity. A continual turnover of slight, 'trendy' music soon jades the palate. The strumming and twang of guitars becomes monotonous if used exclusively. Variety should be the keynote in worship.

The pipe organ for example, still has a vital role to play in church music – it provides a solid and unifying accompaniment to congregational singing, while providing a sustaining and cohesive force in folk styles. It can be used most effectively *with* guitars, combining to produce a dignity of line with rhythmic vitality.

The role of the choir is of paramount importance too. There is a need for a body of people proficient in part singing and voice production to lead the congregation and provide richness and variety in worship. This is not possible with a small guitar group. Again, we need to be all-inclusive in worship and combine every style and resource as part of that ministry of reconciliation. Better still, let us aim for one body of musicians versatile and proficient enough to adapt itself to every musical challenge. The Choir of the Holy Redeemer, Houston, impressed me so much for this very reason. It is an ideal so worth striving for!

In Christ we are set free to enjoy and express the whole of life, not cut ourselves off in isolated corners, feeling threatened when invaded by something outside our normal experience. As whole people we are to embrace every experience and incorporate it into worship. Through this reconciliation, the Church, as in medieval times, can present a unified view of society and the place of the arts within it. We need to show how the arts, and the gift of music in particular, can find their true meaning and perspective in the context of worship.

Commenting on the worship of St. Michael's the Archbishop's Council on Evangelism reported:

> Most important of all, since the subject here is communication of Christ to the world of today, the team pleaded for the continued examination of the most effective blendings of dance, music, movement, drama etc. as expressions of the Word within the Body of Christ . . . Hopefully, as St. Michael's goes on learning how to create the worship services and evangelistic events in which all these things are made one in the Spirit, new levels of Christian communication will be discovered . . . As one member of the dance group commented: 'As dance, touch, non-verbal communication, body-language, all take on a much more vital role in a de-humanised society, so the Church should be a sign of the new creation.'

Church musicians similarly have a prophetic role to make their music 'a sign of the new creation'. All the best of music has its place in worship and strong distinctions between 'classical' and 'pop' are false ones representing a divided society. Only in such manner can the Church claim the ministry of reconciliation and to have a Gospel which relates to 'all sorts and conditions of men'.

Canon Warren sums it up: 'It is an uncomfortable fact that for millions of people in Britain today, the style and content of our church worship is a hindrance, not only to worship, but also to involvement in the body of Christ. It is therefore not a matter of music and worship only; it is also a matter of music and mission.'

5

CHOIR AND MUSIC GROUP

Over the centuries, the choir has been the most common vehicle for leading worship. The way in which the different voices blend together reflects, perhaps more than any other art form, the principles at work within the Body of Christ.

In a study book called *The Worshipping Church* the editors write: 'The choir is the worshipping core at the heart of the body. The members are committed to a whole-hearted involvement in every aspect of the worship event, not simply in singing, but also in listening, offering, caring, sharing, encouraging etc. In a sense, the choir is an established pool of worship into which the rest of the congregation can be drawn and can enrich with their offerings.'

In reality this often seems far from the case. Indeed, many churches have become so disillusioned with the traditional image of the choir that they have abandoned it completely in favour of small vocal/guitar groups more in touch with contemporary trends. In the light of our own experience, this now seems a pity.

In St. Cuthbert's days (1965–1972) we began with nothing! There was no choir, no sung responses and no chanting. What was lacking in musical finesse however, was more than made up by the enthusiastic singing of the congregation. Eventually we developed a small and committed Singing Group of about twelve people with guitar as its basic accompaniment. This was designed to cope with the many new songs being introduced into our fellowship through the renewal movement. The formation of the group coincided with our move into St. Michael's in 1973 and until 1980 proved a source of great encouragement in the development of our worship.

By this time however, the group had begun to lose impetus. Much had been required of a few and it had lost some of its original fervour and commitment. We had become rather cliquish. We also needed to expand our repertoire from largely unison, guitar-type songs to part singing and traditional music.

We were in danger of getting bored! Finally, we needed to identify more with the many churches with which we were continually in contact. While many of these had choirs, few had much vision for worship or idea of how to develop it.

We therefore decided to expand the Singing Group into a choir of some thirty to forty people which would maintain the same quality of worship and fellowship previously experienced, but which would infuse some new life into the old.

In most situations the battle would have been to get the choir and organist to change their ways and emerge into the twentieth century! For us the battle was to persuade the church leaders and congregation that a choir (the word itself conjured up all kinds of bad associations) was not a tool of the devil, subtly planted to hinder the worship of God, but could instead be a stimulating and enriching aid!

So it is today that we have come full circle. We have a choir of some thirty-five people, but it is not an ordinary one. It does not robe or process and many of the membership, which ranges from students to grandparents, do not read music and are only reasonable singers. And yet its music encompasses both classical and contemporary styles and people have consistently improved in technical ability over the years, despite an initial lack of expertise.

But the uniqueness of the group exists in its synthesis of musical and spiritual values. It has a special quality of worship, prayer and mutual care carried over from the Singing Group. This has made the choir an exciting place of growth and development in all aspects.

One young man told me that being in the choir had formed a new pattern and sense of purpose for his life. Others, who entered with much shyness and introversion, have left to say how much they had changed, grown and opened up to God and to other people during their time with us. As one girl put it: 'I do owe a tremendous amount to the fellowship of St. Michael's. Only when in a position to reflect, having left York, did I come to realise how much belonging to the choir had contributed to my feeling more worthwhile as a person. I'm aware that at many times I loathed the choir, feeling useless and a total misfit, but the support and encouragement of many of the members has been of greater value to me than I can ever express!'

Whether we have a choir, a music group or both, there are some important principles to be learnt in the way such groups operate. These profoundly affect the quality of their life and ministry and in turn the life of the whole church. I hope the following principles, learnt over many years, may assist in this.

1) Doing or Being?

I once heard someone remark that 'the effectiveness of what a group does springs from *who* it is.' What are we trying to achieve as a choir or music group and how can we make our ministry as effective as possible? We must strip away all the externals and examine how the group is working. What are its basic aims and motives?

Group dynamics are much talked about these days. Most of the problems in industry or politics stem purely from the poor way in which people relate to each other. Tensions and misunderstandings arise and these hinder the smooth and efficient fulfilment of the task in hand. Just because the task may have a spiritual label does not lessen the importance of good group dynamics or healthy relationships in getting it done. The dynamic in fact provides the foundation for all that the group does and achieves.

The dynamic which Jesus used with his disciples was love. But what is love? It's much more than just a nice feeling, it's really action. We see Jesus loving his disciples by sharing everything with them. They lived their lives together day by day and he shared his deepest feelings with them, calling them to love each other in the same way that they saw him loving them. At the Last Supper, he embarrassed them by doing the slave's task of washing their feet. He said that the world would know that they were his disciples, by the quality of their love.

This heart of love must be at the centre of any group ministry. Without it there is no life. No matter how professional our presentation or even how committed to the task in hand, without a deep commitment to love and care for one another, we will not express the life of God – merely our own human energy. It is the life that we share together which reaches out beyond our words or music to touch and change people. We are frequently far too task-orientated in our approach!

Worship is not created by beautiful organs, choirs or even guitars! Its source is our love for God and for each other. Worship is in fact the fruit of our relationships. When a group tries to lead or encourage worship it is really inviting others to join in the life of worship already

existing within the group. If there is no life in a group's relationships, then, in terms of ministry, it has absolutely nothing to offer. This is hard to accept when we work so hard to perfect our art in the cause of worship. The question is – does it truly reflect who we are, personally and corporately?

2) Calling and Commitment

The leading of worship is a very important role in the corporate life of the church. It is vital that the right people are involved in whatever groups lead it. Tragically, this is very often not the case. Church leaders, organists and choir-masters occupy positions of authority and dictate the form and content of worship with little understanding of what it is about, or sensitivity to the needs of the congregation. Those who lead worship must know that they are called to it by God. As leaders they need spiritual qualifications before musical; indeed, the ordinary members of a group should also share the same sense of calling.

When a person comes forward to join the choir, I give them a short musical audition to check they can sing in tune and will blend with the rest, but I am more interested to find out where a person is spiritually. Do they understand and identify with our worship? How mature are they? Will they fit in with the other members? Could they change? What is God saying to them and to me about their involvement? Are they 'called' to join with us?

Over the years, many have approached me (sometimes with quite dazzling musical talent) to ask to join the choir or singing group. Every time it has been those who had a sense of vocation, an empathy with our worship and a desire to serve who have proved the most loyal, consistent and valuable. Often the 'musicians' have been the awkward ones, hiding behind their instruments, not blending with the other members, becoming threatened and obtuse when asked to do something other than what they wanted. They have lasted a few weeks, during which time they have given a lot of corrective input, but then have left. I now try to look beyond the excellence of the gift, even if it's something we really need, and discover more about the person.

In our early days as a singing group we spelt commitment with a capital 'C'! Everyone was expected to attend the weekly practice and sing at both services on a Sunday as well as the informal fellowship on a Thursday. In addition to this we would also meet for a more extensive prayer and discussion afternoon perhaps every two months. We saw our ministry to be of equal importance with the preaching or teaching of the clergy and if they were required to be there every Sunday, so were we. Members were discouraged from having a casual involvement in the group. There had to be a good reason for being away at a weekend or a major Festival like Easter and, as we were only a dozen in number, every person counted.

Looking back, some of our expectations of people seem a little extreme, particularly for family members. However, at the time the whole church was caught up in the excitement of being involved in something new that God was doing among us and that pioneer feeling enabled us to make the necessary sacrifices to get things off the ground.

One can never get very far in developing the life of a group if one cannot rely on the consistent attendance of the members. There may be three reasons why this commitment is lacking:

a) People may not understand exactly what is required of them. It may never have been spelt out. We have put together a special 'Aims and Duties' Sheet which every choir member is given when they join. It is divided into 'spiritual' and 'practical' and lays down the level of commitment which is expected.*
b) People may not appreciate that the corporate identity and thrust of the group depends vitally on each person offering his own unique gift however large or small.
c) The leader may not be setting a good example.

* See Appendix p. 174.

Experience proves that people rise to the challenge and demand when the aim is worthwhile. The importance of worship should be more than sufficient to justify a high level of commitment in its preparation and execution.

3) Honesty

A group such as a choir offers us the exciting potential of getting to know ourselves and our gifts. This can be a very threatening experience. The pressures of group relationships soon squeeze out what we're really like inside! Anger, resentment, jealousy, all begin to surface and sometimes explode through the veneer of politeness we like to maintain. Consequently, our main fear concerns what others would think if they saw us as we really are. We spend most of our time hiding away behind masks or spiritual fronts.

But where people are loving us, we'll be free to be exactly who we are without fear of rejection. We stop having to pretend in order to be acceptable, or to have everything under control in order to get on with one another.

In a loving and committed group, we can share ourselves and our talents without fear of competitiveness. We won't feel the need to promote our own self-image or our own particular gift because we are accepted just as we are. Jesus never had these problems, he knew who he was. Our problem is often that we have little self-knowledge or self-acceptance. This affects the way we behave and relate to each other. Although we are all sons and daughters of God, we don't feel secure in that relationship. Instead of relating as his children, all equal before him, we relate on the basis of earning acceptance. I'm secure as long as I have a position and know what I'm doing: 'I play the organ, read the lesson, arrange the flowers, I'm the vicar!' Such striving for role or function in search of security destroys a group as a healthy environment for growth and development.

Instead, we must try to see the potential in one another and to do our best to encourage, stimulate and nurture each other's gifts. This is fine when the gift is different from one's own. I have no difficulty encouraging guitarists or other organists in their talents. It's a very different matter when I meet another oboe player, especially one who's better than me!

For some, all this may sound too intense. Why can't we just limit things to the task in hand and get on with it? True, it's possible to keep things ticking over fairly happily on a superficial level. Too much self-examination can become unhealthy. But sooner or later a tension or disagreement will surface and a group not committed to one another very deeply will be difficult to hold together for any length of time. Individuals will polarise into different camps. Some may actually leave while others will just silently cut off from the group deep inside. No one will change or grow through being in the group and its ministry will be non-existent.

Without a commitment to love and be open with one another we will find it impossible to share what we really feel inside about ourselves or others, and very hard to respond to someone who seeks to correct us, even if they desire our good. We must be honest about our reactions and express what we are feeling. For one thing, it is impossible to pray or worship together if there is unresolved tension within the group. Perhaps someone has hurt us with a flippant remark. Maybe someone sings too loud, doesn't concentrate in rehearsals, turns up late or always pushes to the front. It maddens us. If we never tell them, they will never change. At the same time such confrontation without love becomes negative and destructive. With it we grow and mature.

A group must make time to maintain its corporate life.

If there are tensions or unresolved conflicts, it is much better to stop what it's doing and spend time sorting things out. God is love and we are called to be like him and to make love a priority. After the initial trauma, this process brings peace and security within the group. Members are enabled to offer their gifts freely and, in offering them, to find that they are released and used to the full. The music, or whatever else is being accomplished, then becomes an expression of a mature life and inner wholeness which in turn reflects the image of Christ. In our choir it is not unknown for the music practice to be abandoned almost totally in order to sort out a tension or frustration among the membership. Far from wasting time it has cleared the air, brought us much closer together and given us a new impetus in our ministry.

4) Communication and Responsibility

To create and sustain this environment of spiritual life and worship we must continually share and communicate with each other. This requires discipline as it is so easy to slip back into old patterns of relating and leadership. For example, it could be through the individuals in the group simply sharing together what God has been doing or saying in their daily lives. They might link it to a Scripture they have been reading recently or an event in which they saw God at work. In this way a composite picture is built up from each person of what God is saying to the whole group. No one person has a monopoly in this area and it can often be quite remarkable to see how each contribution complements and develops a common theme.

Originally the Singing Group was able to do this as one unit, but when we grew into a choir we had to change the structures to help it happen. We therefore created half a dozen cell or sharing groups within the choir. All choir members gather every fortnight during the practice time to share, support and pray for each other in these groups. The membership of each group is consistent so that people get to know a smaller group of people really well, but about once a year we mix everyone around again. The sharing groups have proved vital to the spiritual life and health of the choir by giving each person a sense of belonging and being cared for.

Another way to involve people is to allow them to discuss the vision and direction the group is taking. Leaders can be very possessive of 'their' ministry. It should not belong to just one individual but should be owned by all. From the beginning of the choir, we gathered the leaders of each sharing group together regularly to oversee its pastoral care. We also decided to create an administrative body in the form of a committee to represent the more practical aspects of the choir's life, but this happened later.

At first I had assumed that the choir could be run on the same casual lines as the Singing Group, that a larger body of people could be just as spontaneous and informal as a small one. I was wrong! Chaotic organisation resulted in much frustration and a breakdown in communication. Fortunately, one of our number volunteered to become choir administrator and assaults were made on punctuality, the planning of rehearsals, creating a proper absence procedure, filing music and organising sectional rehearsals and instrumental workshops.

People are often suspicious of organisation in case it quenches the Spirit, but as long as it serves the vision of the group it can be very liberating. One exciting result was to see the way in which others were drawn into responsibility and we shifted over from 'crisis management' into one which could organise people into jobs previously monopolised by me for the sake of expediency! It always seems easier to do it yourself especially when you haven't thought things through properly and have to do things at the last minute.

Interestingly, after the creation of the committee it became more and more difficult to get the sharing group leaders together to meet. One or two found themselves having to leave the choir and we could not find obvious replacements. Looking back I think God was wanting to teach me a lesson of trust. I had entrusted the spiritual life of the choir to a certain group of people whom I considered spiritually mature, while keeping others in practical roles because I thought them too young or inexperienced. This situation became impossible to maintain and forced me to look to the committee members to fulfil the need for spiritual leadership. Since then we have further opened up the structures and at the moment have a general business meeting to which all members are welcome to come and share their views about the choir's vision and direction.

When people are trusted they flourish and grow. In the choir, when I began to trust people with spiritual and practical responsibility, some of whom I thought were unlikely candidates, we began to see them grow and mature.

5) Pastoral Concern and Leadership

A friend of mine once remarked that leading a choir was 10% musical and 90% pastoral. When it comes down to it, it is all about the way we handle people.

Often we can look on the people we have in our church as so many gifts on a talent register. Some ministers are constantly thinking how they can use the latest song or drama to fit in with their sermon. If that is our only thought, people will soon feel 'used' and not valued as people. We need to be careful that the ministry we are involved in doesn't violate and pressurise its members by its demands. We must take account of each other's families, home and work situations. We are whole people and the whole person must be cared for. In a group such as a choir, where there is a high demand of commitment and dedication, we should always have an eye to the price that is being paid perhaps by the wife or children at home.

The way to avoid these difficulties is to be involved in the pastoral care of each member, meeting them as friends and not as 'talents'. It's good to look to the social side of the group, having parties from time to time, drawing spouses into the life of the group, sharing meals and baby-sitting for one another. We shouldn't always be work orientated. This way the group can go a long way to creating a healthy family atmosphere which, in turn, will greatly enhance its ministry.

Good leadership determines how much growth and maturity takes place in a group. It affects its whole approach to ministry and also its ability to perform and perfect the practical side of what it does. People are more willing to work hard and pull together, to learn notes and improve voices for example. They will come together for extra practices without too much complaint and will really take on the responsibility for the ministry as their own. I have been amazed at the commitment and loyalty of my own choir members, particularly at times when I thought the pressures of time and activity would be too much for them.

Of course, the leader must also exercise a directive role, especially in music. Practices need to start punctually (as somebody once said: 'The trouble about being punctual is that there is never anyone around to appreciate it!'); the leader needs to make the best use of the time by planning ahead what the group needs to accomplish during that rehearsal; he needs to ensure high standards and proper concentration in rehearsal and performance; he must maintain the vision and commitment of the group and teach people to be sensitive to one another. Sometimes he will need to discipline people who are not doing the right thing. Maybe a person begins to disrupt the life or ministry of the group or to pull away from the original vision. For the sake of the group as a whole the leader must not be afraid to stand up for what he believes God has called him and the group to do. However, if he has earned their trust and respect, this will be easier for him.

In the Singing Group we operated a shared leadership of two. I took the musical side while my friend Phil took on the pastoral side. We would meet every week to talk and pray about things and our joint leadership added authority, sensitivity and corporateness to our ministry. When the group expanded into the choir we continued this shared leadership through the group leaders and the committee. This continues to provide a broad base for leadership and avoids the pitfalls of a one-person monopoly.

Shared leadership has other advantages. It has been said that a group takes on the characteristics and personality of its leader. To share leadership with others takes some of the horror out of this fact, though I must confess to seeing some of my own tastes and prejudices being reflected in some of the members of the choir!

For this reason, it is very important that a leader is humble about his gifts and is as honest as he can be about his motives and aims in leadership. In very subtle ways, we can end up building private empires in the name of Christian ministry.

The leader is given authority to lead by the group. It is a gift, not a right, and he is there to serve and enable, not dominate. It will be a test of the leader's maturity and wholeness to see how far he is able to do this. If a person is given the gift of leadership, then the others must submit to him and do all they can to support and encourage him.

I remember with shame sitting in the woodwind department of the orchestra and tearing the conductor to pieces behind the security of my music stand. It was a very different story when I tried my hand at conducting and realised how difficult it was! It is so easy to criticise leaders from a passive, back-row position. Leadership is a two-way thing however, and requires the active co-operation of all parties to become a creative and releasing thing.

Ideally, the leader should constantly be trying to do himself out of a job! He is not there to do everything himself because 'he knows best'. How can other people develop their gifts if they are never given the opportunity to have a go at conducting or playing for example, because the leader is always in the limelight? Sometimes we may monopolise things because we are frightened of not producing the best each time. But if perfection is our goal, then we should ask ourselves what God's priorities are in ministry or worship. If I, as a leader, am doing my job properly, I should be able to leave and expect the group to continue to function quite adequately for a long time after my departure. The leader must trust that God is well able to use the people in his charge and having given them responsibility must be very careful that he doesn't take things back again.

The authority that we have as leaders stems from our lives. Jesus had enormous authority because he was what he claimed to be. He did what he expected others to do. If we want to produce love and care in a group we must begin by being loving and caring ourselves. It's no good teaching about it at arm's length and expecting results. Similarly, if we want an openness and honesty to develop within the group we lead, we must begin by being open and honest about our own thoughts and feelings.

Some people think it very wrong for a leader to share his weakness, but experience has taught us that to be vulnerable and honest as leaders earns enormous respect and elicits a great response from others. They realise that leaders are human beings too, and that if God can use him or her in leadership then he can use me too!

6) Worship and Prayer

On alternate weeks, when we are not sharing in small groups, we spend the equivalent time in worship and prayer together as a whole choir. Unless we ourselves learn to worship we have no hope of leading others. (Group sharing and general worship times can in fact account for almost half of the two and a half hour weekly practice*).

Through our worship and prayer we are cementing our lives together and asking God to equip and use us. We are acknowledging that without his help we can achieve nothing of spiritual value. This preparation is also carried over to Sunday when we meet at least three quarters of an hour before each service to get ready through prayer and practice.

In the Old Testament the choir would often be sent out ahead of the army to proclaim the supremacy of the God of Israel and to invoke his power (2 Chr. 20:21–24). It made them extremely vulnerable to attack! We too have often found ourselves under attack as we have exercised our ministry both as a choir and as a singing group before it.

The worship is the visible focus of the church's life. It is also a powerful weapon in the spiritual armament against the forces of evil. In worship we are lifting up the name of Jesus as a banner and proclaiming his lordship. It is

* See Typical Practice Schedule, Appendix p. 176

inevitable that as leaders of worship we should experience something of this spiritual battle too. Sometimes it
may take the form of sickness, sometimes apathy or
depression. Other times it may come in the form of
negative criticism from the very people we are seeking to
serve. We must learn to put on all the spiritual armour
(Eph. 6:10–18).

Whatever the source of our difficulties and problems,
they throw us back upon God and make us realise that we
need his help. Someone once said to me that if we ever
lost a sense of holy fear and weakness in our ministry it
was time to give up. We would no longer be relying upon
God. By making worship and prayer a priority we ensure
that we stay within the sphere of the Spirit's activity and
remain useable.

6

CREATIVE MUSIC

God's Holy Spirit is a creative spirit, so wherever God is at work there will be new life, new creativity. At creation itself we are told that the 'Spirit of God was moving over the face of the waters'. And of course at Pentecost the Holy Spirit brought the Church to birth, giving it the power to witness to the living Jesus.

Another well known reference to the Spirit of God occurs in Ezekiel 37 where the prophet is set down in a valley full of dry bones. He is commanded to prophesy to the bones and they begin to come together. Sinews, flesh and skin cover them but they have no 'breath' in them. He is then told to prophesy to the breath: 'Come from the four winds, O breath, and breathe upon these slain that they may live.' The breath comes into them and they become a vast number of living human beings. God tells Ezekiel that the dry bones are the house of Israel scattered in exile and cut off from their homeland. He encourages them saying: 'I will put my Spirit within you, and you shall live, and I will place you in your own land. Then you shall know that I, the Lord, have spoken, and I have done it, says the Lord.'

I mention this particular passage because it is not unlike our situation today. We are meant to be the 'Body of Christ' but seem in many places to be just so many dry, unconnected and lifeless bones. We could hardly be thought of as a living body, supple, versatile and full of energy, ready to move and act and affect its circumstances. But there is hope. Whenever the Church has become dry or lifeless in the past, God's Spirit has brought renewal and new life. It may not be in the way or the place that we expected but it has been an undeniable movement of God.

Successive revivals over the centuries have brought people back to experience again the original power of the Gospel and to re-establish a proper balance of its ingredients. The Reformation corrected many abuses in the Church and opened up the scriptures for the ordinary man to understand. The Methodist Revival in the eighteenth century brought thousands back to a personal faith, again through a fresh understanding of the Scriptures. Pentecostalism at the turn of the century saw a return of the power and gifts of the Spirit to the Church. Recently, the Charismatic Movement has seen that power invade the traditional denominations. The idea of the Body of Christ has become meaningful on a local level. St. Paul's instructions on the operation of spiritual gifts have become particularly relevant. Many, many people within the denominations have experienced a release of new power and energy in their lives. Perhaps the most significant fruit of this current renewal has been an incredible movement towards unity and reconciliation between ordinary Christians of very different traditions, brought together by this common experience of God. Music has often had a part in this. Indeed, where doctrine and theology divide the denominations, music unites. Its common language, which goes right across the board, is one of the most potent binding forces in current renewal.

Wherever there has been a renewal of the Church's life there has also been a burst of new creativity. This has expressed itself in art and architecture, but especially in music. Hymns and songs have sprung up as people have sought to express their new-found joy and freedom in Christ. Eventually, these have been assimilated into the hymnody of the established Church. What we some-times forget is that those who originally sang about being 'lost in wonder, love and praise' really were! We can often sing or listen to church music today without ever entering into the intense spiritual experience which first prompted the composer to put pen to paper. I find it amusing that cultured audiences can blandly listen to Bach's cantatas when their words, particularly when translated, are so personal and so emotional – two qual-ities of religion generally frowned upon in such circles.

But personal experience is vital to creativity, especially in worship. One of the reasons for the lack of renewal in church art or music over recent decades, particularly on a local level, must surely come from the dearth of spiritual life in its people. It is so significant that wherever renewal has touched a group of Christians they have begun to compose new songs, create new dances or design new banners to express their experience. The Holy Spirit creates an overflow of life which demands expression in one form or another. It may be simple and often naive but it is so genuine and so in touch with the initial experience.

This has certainly been true of St. Michael's. Many of us in those early days came into a new experience of the Holy Spirit which released us in many areas of our lives, but particularly in our emotions. We could sing confi-dently of the love of God in familiar hymns because we really loved him. We could raise our arms in worship or embrace the person next to us because a greater force overcame our shyness and embarrassment. Like Jacob, God touched each one of us and made us vulnerable to him and to each other. This weakness became our strength because we began to discover that we were part of one another in the Body of Christ and that each one of us had a special gift which fitted into the whole. Every person was needed if the Body was to function properly and every member was equally important. The musicians began to see their ministry as of equal importance with the ministries of preaching, teaching or pastoral work. Each one was equally inspired by the Spirit and required that those who ministered to the Body maintained their own personal spiritual life.

In worship, new songs were introduced in our fellowship meetings which could interpret more effectively the new sense of freedom and informality that a living body required. They needed to be simple and easy to pick up without a lot of fuss. At first we drew on the resources of renewal groups that had already sprung up elsewhere in places like America and New Zealand. It was obvious from their simplicity that these had been produced by local congregations who were sharing our experience and our need. We began to follow their example and to compose our own songs which uniquely expressed the life we had together in York. We used what was appropriate from other sources and filled in the gaps with our own material.

The Singing Group, as it was then, provided an excellent testing ground for the new compositions. No one had exalted or grandiose ideas of what was or was not acceptable; we could try things out to see if they worked. It was generally left up to the individuals to produce new material if they felt inspired, perhaps by a significant teaching or event within the fellowship, or in their personal lives. We had no organised composing group or any means of encouraging or improving on our first attempts beyond trial and error. It was all rather hit and miss.

It is worth saying at this point that I have never viewed myself as a very creative person. Like many classical musicians, I was lost without a piece of paper to read from and very threatened by the prospect of improvising or composing anything. The classical music tradition lays enormous emphasis on perfection and originality. Unless a composer can create a completely original style and has attained considerable stature in the music world, he is not worth bothering with. Plagiarism is definitely frowned on. Handel, Telemann and their contemporaries on the other hand, thought nothing of borrowing great chunks of material from one another's works.

The copyright laws make such practice quite out of the question today! Each composer must strive to express himself in a unique personal style, different from everyone else. The avant garde has flourished in the pursuit of these aims, with people creating ever more outrageous pieces in order to be thought original. I have listened to a university lecturer rattling a number of differently pitched plastic flower pots on the concert hall floor and to a piano piece by the American composer John Cage which involved playing the same note with varying degrees of intensity for some ten minutes. (The music department Steinway was never quite the same after that!). Where was the middle ground? I couldn't identify with the newest trends as they seemed so ridiculous, nor could I attain the genius of the 'greats'. I therefore assumed that to be a creative musician you had to have something extra-special which I had not. I decided that performing was a safer bet and left composing to the experts or the eccentrics!

That was until I became deeply involved with the people at church. Music was on a much more practical and functional level. It didn't pretend to be great art but it did express the emotion and response of the people. It seemed that it had gained a sensible perspective of what it was meant to be. In a way, it was like medieval art. The composer or artist was not a great and awesome spirit wrestling with the universe and producing great masterpieces in the process. He was the servant of God and of the society in which he was placed.

For me, music found a new meaning and purpose. I began to learn to improvise on my oboe in times of worship. Our composers, though very humble and using familiar idioms, were expressing something fresh and unique. Everyone got a thrill from performing a new song written specially for us. No one worried if the melody or chord progression bore similarities to other pieces; if it was meaningful and relevant in our circumstances, what did it matter?

In 1978 a New Zealander arrived in York to study composition at the university and to join our fellowship. His name was Christopher Norton. He was described in a newspaper cutting sent to me by a friend as a 'brilliant young composer'. I found the description a little offputting and wondered what on earth would turn up on our doorstep! In fact Chris proved to be a God-send. Although a classical pianist, who had appeared with the national orchestra, he also played keyboards for a leading Gospel band. He had also had a lot of experience in schools encouraging children in creative composition.

Chris' gifts were ideal for our situation. Soon after his arrival he got together a small group of us to begin sharing and evaluating our compositions. Our first meeting took place in the back room of the rectory on a hot sunny Saturday afternoon. Chris got us working straight away and off the top of his head gave us four simple lines to set to a tune:

Praise the Lord in the heavens,
Praise the Lord all the earth,
Let your hearts magnify him,
Clap your hands and sing for joy.

He told us to take them away to different parts of the

house and garden and to come back in half an hour with a simple tune. Beating back the panic we wondered what on earth we could do. We were a pretty diverse group in terms of musical taste and this became apparent when we returned and shared one by one what we had put together.

It was an amazing experience to hear so many completely different approaches to the same group of words. Some people had set them in a rock guitar style, others had folk-like melodies. Mine was reminiscent of an 'O' level music paper – I had so many do's and don'ts to contend with that it made my song boringly predictable!

Chris, however had a good word to say about all of them and was so good at drawing out the musical implications of each attempt, putting in or touching up the harmony and giving the appropriate rhythmic accompaniment on the piano. Each person felt they had achieved something special which they could begin to develop and improve. No one was made to feel inadequate or foolish or that they had nothing to offer. The workshop offered hope, especially to those of us who were so self-conscious about anything we composed and were always worried about what the professionals might think!

Since then we have had many such composition groups and I have tried the approach myself at conferences, usually giving people a simple communion text to set. Always, the material people produce, sometimes singly, sometimes in pairs, surprises one by its freshness and originality and by the variety of styles in which people compose. Even at the most local level, in a country church, a group of young children, teenagers and a few adults produced a similar variety, of which several compositions would have been quite suitable for congregational use.

The thrill and excitement of creating one's own music

cannot be measured. Nothing can compare with it, not even the great classics. It belongs to that particular group of people for that time. At one conference I held, a professional singer, who had just left a very famous singing group, found the experience of composing his own little song quite revolutionary. He had never done it before in his whole life. For most classical musicians the thought of composing is quite unthinkable, it never enters a person's head!

The same can be true in the Church. We are constantly looking to the professionals to provide us with our music for worship but never think that the Holy Spirit might inspire some of those in our midst. We look outside for inspiration, even to the non-Christian who has no commitment to, or identification with our worship. When we think about using an anthem we draw on our excellent heritage from the past, or the latest publication in the *Musical Times*. It never occurs to us that we might have the potential to write a very creditable anthem under our very noses. When we think about producing a new hymn-book we commission a number of highly respected individuals to compose a selection of new hymns for congregational use. The fact that these individuals may not have had their material tried and tested in a local worship situation and may not even understand the needs of those they are writing for, does not seem to bother editors. Dreariness and a feeling of prefabrication in melody, harmony and lyrics is a common result.

Yet we as the Church possess the Creative Spirit in full measure as we operate together. In our own musical life in York the few of us who are professionals have been able to cooperate with the many amateurs. God has given them the initial spark of creativity and we have been able to make their material performable and useful in worship. The experts have made their gifts available for the benefit of the whole body and together we have gone infinitely further than we would have individually.

Many of our composers have had no formal musical training whatsoever. One young man composes on his bicycle as he rides to work. Often a phrase from his Bible reading, or a recent teaching has impressed him and he begins to turn it over in his mind. He then comes home and sings it on to a cassette while he still remembers it and then later works the chords out on his guitar. One song was prompted by the difficulties of being a Christian in a secular job and took the Beatitudes as its theme.

Another girl got a preliminary grade on the clarinet while still at school. When she joined the choir she thought the composition group was a glorified theory lesson on how to write down music. The experience prompted her to begin composing her own songs. The results have been marvellous and she has discovered a natural gift for writing beautiful, evocative melodies with very original characteristics.

Someone else presents his songs without any accompaniment at all! He has them all written out in pencil in a large book. As he sings the music is full of rhythm and vitality. The style is easily identifiable as coming from various rock or pop sources but the actual melodies and form of the songs are again, very unusual. Recently he has begun to learn the piano by ear and has written a very expressive and emotionally charged song about the Way to the Cross. It is full of major sevenths and jagged rhythms which capture the starkness and brutality of the scene in an imaginative way.

I could go on and on describing the incredible variety of songs which has come from this ordinary group of people, or the thrill and excitement we have all received when the bare bones of words and melody have been dressed with harmony and different instruments and the piece performed for the first time. It belongs to all of us and expresses the life we share as members of the same body, each working together for the common good. True enough, Chris and myself have provided the expertise in arrangement and performance, but it makes me think that similar results could be produced in almost any situation. Think of how many young people now play instruments and are actively involved in music making, either classical or pop. Think of how many professional musicians and teachers there are spread all over the country. The trouble is, they are not within the body of the Church, or if they are, they are unable to cope with or encourage a creative approach to music and are too hidebound by the traditional view.

The approach we have to creativity very much depends on our presuppositions – what we think of as acceptable or unacceptable in worship. For us, a simpler approach has meant that many others have been able to offer their own songs in worship. A lowering of our cultural sights makes it possible to begin. If we are aiming to copy Bach, Beethoven and the like, it is hopeless, we migh as well give up. But with small beginnings, instead of saying 'We couldn't possible do that!' we begin to realise the possibility that 'Yes, we could!'

The love and acceptance we experience as a small group of composers are also important factors in helping us to offer our humble first attempts. To create a song, a dance, or a banner, and then share it is such an exposing thing. An insensitive, critical remark can quickly stunt or destroy a person's gift altogether. Competitiveness or comparison can easily produce a fear of what others may think – this also stunts creativity.

From humble beginnings our composings have continued to develop. Many of the songs have been recorded on various albums from the church, and out of four recordings so far, the vast majority of songs have been our own. These represent a wide variety of styles from children's songs to anthems. In fact we called our little recording company 'Mustard Seed Recordings' – not inappropriately as it turned out!

A further development has been in the creation of large scale presentations or musicals where different composers have contributed material to develop a particular theme. I have written more extensively about this in my book *Using the Bible in Music**.

Our first attempt was to put something together with readings of Scripture and poetry on the subject of Pentecost. Using the first four chapters of the Book of Acts, we divided them into various sections and people took different parts to compose songs about. Some songs used the Biblical text while others were a free interpretation of the general meaning or significance. The event itself took place on a Saturday to an audience drawn from the congregation and was very well received. It proved quite short however, and only lasted about fifty minutes.

From this first attempt, the natural progression was to develop the themes of Christmas and Easter. Because of the initial success, these presentations took the place of our Sunday evening worship a week or two before each festival. We took care to provide more congregational involvement spreading hymns and carols throughout. The final form was reminiscent of a Bach Passion with its mix of congregational hymns, choral pieces and solo arias. Some pieces unfolded the narrative while others were reflections or meditations on the different parts.

Our initial hope for these presentations was to include more of the other art forms. (We have dance and drama groups in the church.) Unfortunately this proved too difficult to do at first. However, as we approached the York Festival in 1984, we were looking for some sort of musical presentation to offer which would express the

* Bible Society; publ. 1983; No. 10.

life and ministry of our fellowship. As the Festival embraced Whitsun, a revamping of our Pentecost musical, this time including dance and drama, was an obvious choice. We decided to call it 'Acts' and to develop its various sections more extensively. Two humorous sketches were written from within the groups, one or two more songs were specially written and dances were created to interpret the coming of the Spirit. Because we wanted there to be an element of worship in the performance we also included familiar songs from our Sunday repertoire from other outside sources. The nature of the performance precluded the use of traditional hymns.

The event was staged for four evenings in our church and involved building a stage in the chancel, blacking out the building and rigging up professional lights and P.A. It was quite an expensive venture but over a thousand people came to the performances and 'Acts' received very favourable reviews and comments. It was an excellent way of drawing visitors and outsiders into the church and communicating our life and our message in an enjoyable and un-threatening way.

Since then we have taken the presentation on a choir trip to Sweden where it again proved an invaluable way of communicating the life we share as a church. It remains to be seen what developments the future holds in store. I would like to see our composers working more to order and turning their attention to setting various parts of the liturgy and to creating some new hymns and more simple worship songs for example.

Above all we must continue to be true to our own personal experience of God, remaining open and available to his Spirit. Our gifts can then interpret his activity richly and creatively in all our lives.

7

MOVING FORWARD TOGETHER: QUESTIONS AND ANSWERS

In the early years of St. Cuthbert's, the development of the music and worship lagged behind other things for a long time. The organist was unsympathetic but it was decided that, in love, we should continue to pray about the situation and wait for a natural change.

Meanwhile, we found our informal fellowship meeting a good place to experiment with new forms of worship. No one had preconceived ideas of what should happen and it was a much less threatening place for the musicians and worship leaders if they made mistakes. Much of the spiritual life of the church was nurtured here through the teaching, the prayer and the early exercising of spiritual gifts.

When the organist eventually resigned seven years later, we were just at the right stage of development to begin introducing some of our new experience into public worship. The Family Service proved an excellent place for experimentation and here things developed more rapidly with the introduction of a vocal group, a children's orchestra and some new children's songs, sometimes with dance. The Evening Service took longer to be influenced but we soon decided to gather all the interested parties together and have a day away to discuss the formation of a music group which could lead the whole of our worship in a more organised fashion.

David Watson gave some teaching on worship and its significance in the life of the Church today and also on the qualities required of those who lead it. We discussed our own church situation and our musical needs. If we continued with a singing group, how many should it involve, what would be its commitment, who would lead it, what would be its aim and vision? We spent some time in prayer together asking God to guide us and help people to know whether they should be involved or not.

In this way we were able to move forward together with the backing of the whole church and its leadership. The following questions and answers may help you decide whether now is the right moment for you to move forward in your worship.

1) Sorting Priorities

There are many important priorities which a church faces at different times. It may be that evangelism or pastoral concern are particular priorities at the moment. There is certainly a danger in trying to do too many things and thereby doing nothing well! We can tend to flit from one new thing to another, never seeing anything through to maturity and completion.

However, if our worship life is flourishing, many of these other areas will open up naturally as a result. We have seen how worship can be a very effective evangelistic agent. Worship also opens and softens people to acknowledge their needs and reach out to God.

If we do need to look at our worship, then we must count the cost. Traditional outlooks and ways of doing things may need to be altered. We may need to change round the furniture of the church to make it more conducive to corporate worship. Present musical structures may have to be abandoned if these are no longer fulfilling our needs. Perhaps a smaller, more informal group of musicians would be more suitable than the remnant of a once glorious robed choir. A good piano might be a better substitute for the wheezy old organ which is now on its last legs and which we cannot afford to refurbish. Maybe we should consider employing a 'musical director' to nurture our music and draw new musical gifts into worship, rather than pursue the fruitless search for a suitable organist? Perhaps the minister will have to give up his cherished right to determine what does or does not happen in worship so that others may take responsibility? Maybe the organist will have to give up the birthright to rule as musical tyrant and be willing to let the guitar make an appearance or allow the congregation the latest choruses they've been chafing to sing?

2) Vision

Proverbs 29:18 says: 'Where there is no vision the people perish.' We need some sort of vision or plan in order to move forward. To find this we must, above all, pray and seek God's will for our situation. It is no good importing good ideas and gimmicks expecting things to happen as a result. They will never be a true reflection of the Body of Christ where we are. We need the Holy Spirit to accomplish renewal and it must start within each one of us personally. If we are not free to express an intimate worship of God personally, we cannot expect it to happen corporately.

Nor is this a vision which can be formulated by one person who then presses ahead, assuming people will fall in behind – they don't. A vision must be owned by everyone and it can only come through corporate prayer and discussion where we each seek to know God's mind together and contribute our little pieces of the jigsaw. Too often the vicar or organist comes up with a new idea and tries to impose it on everybody without laying it open for discussion first.

3) Supportive Leadership

It is one thing to have a vision if you are an ordinary member of the congregation, but quite another to put it into effect if your vicar or organist does not share it! One often hears of people who are so frustrated because they find the leaders of their church uncooperative or mis-understanding in an area they would like to see im-proved. Yet without the full backing and covering of the leaders there is little chance of any renewal of worship really growing and maturing. Ministers and organists are indeed the kingpins. They may benignly allow you your little bit of freedom, perhaps by starting a prayer group or playing the guitar in the family service, but if they really do not share your vision things will soon return to their original state. All you can do is pray.

On the other hand, you may be the minister who wants to see the worship develop but are having difficulty getting others to understand it. It might be good in this situation to begin teaching about worship so that people can begin to grasp what you are getting at; that it's not just your good idea. It would be most important to try to win over the organist and choir and also the church council. You could organise a discussion day perhaps with a visiting speaker outlining the vision of worship and how music fits in. There should be some place for questions and come-back. You could try to get as much interaction between the different parties to allay fear and misgivings. Ask them how they see the worship developing and if they see any particular difficulties or frustrations. You might send the strategic people on a music in worship conference or to visit another church where people could catch the vision of what you have in mind.

4) Making Love Your Aim

Be careful how you do things. Without a spirit of love, in the end we accomplish nothing for God's kingdom. Love forms people and helps them to change and soften. Pestalozzi wrote: 'To change people you must love them. Your influence extends only as far as your love.' This will mean exercising great patience if you encounter stubbornness and unreasonable reaction; also giving much encouragement to people very unsure of their gifts and talents in new areas.

Do not judge people or situations out of hand. I remember leading a weekend music workshop for one church and being collared by the vicar's wife on the very first evening. She gave me a 'who's who' of the choir and congregation: who was going to respond, who was not. When it came to it I found the so-called 'dyed in the wool' traditionalists some of the most open and sympathetic to what was being said. Funnily enough, it was the vicar's wife who was the main cause of all the problems!

We must not presume to know how people will react to change and innovation. At another weekend workshop I did with a small team, an old monocled lady sat three pews back, reminiscent of the old countess in the film *Murder on the Orient Express* (furs included!). As we sang and played some of our new songs in the service we all wondered how she would take it. As she left she had a word with the vicar in one of the team's hearing: 'I shall *not* be coming next week,' she said. 'It will be too . . . boring!' When introducing new things we expect the worse and often become defensive. Our uncertainty and insecurity over the thing we are introducing sometimes makes us come over very strong and aggressive. It is therefore important to realise this and to be open with people and to explain exactly what we have in mind and the reasons for doing it. We may need to spend some time with them beforehand preparing the ground. To sweep aside someone's feelings on the basis of a lack of spirituality for example, is not loving. All of us have a lot of fear of the unknown, especially as we grow older. No change is worthy of Christ if it violates people. I always find the example of the Church of the Redeemer in Houston helpful. As the organist wrote:

> During the first five years of renewal, no changes were made in the Sunday liturgy. A plainsong mass was sung and Anglican chants used for the psalms at the Sunday Eucharist. Graham, the rector, required that the *people* be changed rather than their circumstances. Despite the fact that our form of worship did not change, there was a difference in our services arising out of our shared life: a warmth pervaded the church services. As a deeper awareness of God developed, the people began to embrace the liturgy as their own.

It is the kind of people we are and the kind of fellowship we have that is all-important. We must decide what sort and what degree of change is necessary to enable this to develop most efficiently. We may also have to make the hard decision of telling a person or group of people that we have listened to their objections honestly and openly but that, for the sake of the whole, we must move forward. If they then react and withdraw we can at least be reassured that we have tried to accommodate them and been loving towards them. What we must not do is answer back from anger, bitterness or frustration, or vacillate and fail to have the courage of our convictions. As far as we can, we must try to ensure that the whole church moves forward together, particularly in the realm of worship, and that no parties and splits develop.

5) Changing a Situation

'Nothing ever happens in our church. If things don't change soon I'm leaving!'

This is a common enough feeling among people who have had some experience of renewal but who find no outlet or support in their local church. They have had a word with the vicar about their experience but have met with polite resistance. Some members of the church council are openly hostile.

David Watson used to say: 'If you want life – give your life; if you want prayer – give your prayer; if you want worship – give your worship.' It is most important that we don't criticise from the touchline without ever getting involved in practical service. There are many people who serve only themselves in worship, going from place to place to find what suits them. This can be specially true of 'charismatics' who may well have had a new experience of God, but who immediately criticise and pull down others who don't appear to share their experience or enthusiasm. Other people are treated as second class citizens or as ignorant and unspiritual.

This hardly encourages the cause of renewal and it is something to guard against. The better way to encourage change and a sympathetic response is to show love and support in practical ways – becoming the most loyal, most committed individual or group in the church for example. I heard of a family who returned to a small parish in Ireland having been involved for some time in a very lively church in England. The priest did not share their enthusiasm for renewal and was very suspicious. Verbal argument and suggestion got nowhere in encouraging change so the family decided to take a different approach. They began to help the priest in all sorts of practical ways – doing his washing, making him cakes and biscuits, cleaning his car. In one year the priest was a changed man; in two the whole parish had changed!

Always try to be understanding of another's position. Your particular experience of renewal may not be unique. God may choose to renew different people in different ways. Who are you to judge which is the best? Perhaps the vicar doesn't know how to share responsibility and feels threatened when others make suggestions. The church council or elders may have no first-hand experience of renewed worship and fear the rumours of division, strife and emotional excess which they've heard about. Maybe, back in 1970, someone went on a conference and came back speaking in tongues, causing major confusion and dissension in the church. You were not around at the time, but the memory is still fresh for some older members. An understanding and mature approach may help to make vicars, council members, organists, more ready to receive your message.

6) Awkward Organists

One is always hearing of organists who appear to present major difficulties to the advancement of worship in church. The organist thinks the new music is just so much rubbish. He is deeply suspicious and is unwilling to co-operate. The poor performance of charismatic 'ditties' by ragged groups with out of tune instruments confirms his prejudices. As often the only trained musician in the church he, of course, always has the upper hand in any argument. He may be quite right, too!

All will depend on having a common ground of Christian commitment. A person may be spiritually sensitive but express this differently from ourselves. Others, frankly, have little interest in the spiritual and are there more for the music. With one there will be basic unity of spirit and an openness to God; with the other, forging a new vision for worship together will be impossible. In discerning, we should be careful not to pre-judge a person but be very sensitive in the way we put new ideas across.

We can, for example, presume from the start that a person won't understand what we are trying to do and this makes matters worse. Instead we must try to understand his reactions. Maybe he or she is too old to change and adapt to modern styles. He may feel threatened and out of his depth because he just doesn't have the musical expertise to cope. In this situation it might be possible to confine him to his organ playing and the traditional elements in the service and get a younger person to lead the more modern parts. Sometimes we may have to be honest enough to say that the time has now come for him to retire.

Sometimes his antagonism may be caused by feelings of isolation. The minister and other leaders may need to encourage him and lend their support in increasing membership of the choir for example, or by letting him have some say in the choosing of hymns. Vicars often complain about the obstinacy and awkwardness of their organists but may well be treating them badly, riding rough-shod over their feelings and making high-handed decisions without consulting them. The vicar's attitude betrays the fact that he is not treating the organist as an equal in ministry and this quickly elicits a childish response. Trust and respect are soon reciprocated.

7) Difficult Choirs

The choir objects to any new changes in their musical repertoire. 'What's wrong with what we've got? We don't need to change,' they say. The choir is an intimidating group of people. It has 'organised' and is prepared for battle! It will take on vicars, church-wardens, congregations, even organists if they disagree with the way things are going. Sometimes the choir can represent one of the biggest blocks to the growth of worship and spiritual life in a church. No wonder some ministers are only too glad to disband it and get rid of it altogether. But what a pity to lose a body of people capable of enriching and enhancing worship if they have the right approach and attitude.

If you are a choir member standing up for your rights and resisting change, think for a minute about your motives. Surely you are there primarily to serve the needs of the congregation and to provide the musical lead which is going to be best for them. The Scriptural principle applies that if we hold on too hard to our rights, we are likely to lose them altogether (Luke 17:33). If we keep a loose hold on the things we treasure most we are more likely to preserve them.

If you are in the position of trying to win over your choir or organist you might consider building some bridges. Firstly, if they are short of numbers, why not join their ranks and try to infiltrate with love and practical support? If you are a minister, it might be good to involve yourself in choir practices, perhaps singing, but also by providing some spiritual input in the form of a short teaching or a time of prayer about the music or Sunday worship. Alternatively, if you are the music leader, why not arrange some of the new worship material chorally, or use arrangements already in existence? If you choose well, you could provide a musical challenge equal to some of the traditional repertoire and earn respect and understanding for contemporary styles. You could also help the choir to understand the new music by playing good quality recordings to them so that they can hear the music as it should be. It is very difficult to gauge the quality and effect of a simple chorus in terms of its value in worship when looking at it on the printed page. Many of the songs need a live setting to make sense.

8) Lack of Resources

People often complain that they have a dearth of musical talent, which is hindering their progress in worship. 'We've been trying for years to get an organist but we've never had any lasting success.' Maybe you are looking in the wrong direction! Few people are taking up the organ these days for various reasons, and it may be more sensible to look to pianists or guitarists to satisfy your musical needs. One vicar in the Dales uses his flute to lead congregational singing. The most ridiculous situation of all is to have talented musicians sitting idle in the pews because we have decided that only the organ is suitable for accompanying worship!

It is good to remember that this instrument has had a very chequered career in the Church, frequently being banned altogether! Perhaps we should try to get back to the eighteenth-century minstrel's gallery when a variety of instruments was used to lead worship.

We must start from where we are. Frequently we spend all our time looking towards stage three or four, envying the music and musicians of other churches and dismissing our own attempts as worthless. Everyone has to begin somewhere. If you are in a country situation, you might think of inviting local school children in to help accompany your worship, or sing. You might even invite non-churchgoers to give some instrumental help if this were appropriate. I know of villages where this has happened. One would obviously have to take the spiritual lead and guard priorities but sometimes we can be very narrow in whom we do or do not allow to join us. As long as we hold the initiative it could be a reasonable compromise.

Another common complaint concerns the level of expertise amongst local musicians. The organist or pianist is of the 'reluctant' sort, very few of the singers read music and no one feels confident to lead the choir or music group. Perhaps the guitarists are not too good at tuning their instruments. Here is a good opportunity to produce a real team effort!

If the keyboard player does not feel able to lead the group, perhaps the minister or a lay-reader could look after the leadership and spiritual life of the group, while the former corrects notes and provides accompaniment.

In time they may feel confident enough to take on more responsibility when they are more mature. If instrumental technique is the difficulty, why not invest in an electronic tuner for the guitarists? This could save time tuning up! You could also get people to attend evening classes or private tuition to become more proficient in their skills.

'He who is faithful in a very little, is faithful also in much' (Luke 16:10). Begin with what you've got, praying for God's guidance and provision. You can tackle the Bach cantata the year after next. In the meantime, satisfy yourself with providing an adequate and tidy accompaniment for congregational needs.

9) We're Stuck!

From time to time a music group, or a whole church, will lose its way in worship. People feel they cannot get any further with each other. They have become tired, jaded and weary of their ministry. This was our feeling towards the end of our time as a singing group. We seemed to have run down. It was time for a change. Significantly, it was the musicians who first noticed the malaise. I'm sure the congregation would have been quite happy to continue with the same musical lead ad infinitum but this only increased our feelings of isolation, misunderstanding, of being 'used' and not supported.

We decided to open up the whole subject of our music and worship for general discussion. I prepared a short paper outlining some of the causes and needs which I felt and distributed it to the church leadership. I talked it over with them and we decided to test the general feeling. As a result, we expanded the ministry, forming a larger choir and through this, gave the opportunity for much new, fresh blood to be introduced. The whole process revitalised us and we are still going strong!

It may be that you could initiate a similar process of discussion and evaluation, whether you are just starting to renew your worship, or have been underway for some time but are now feeling stuck. Throw everything up for grabs. It might give the opportunity for everyone, whether organist or long-standing choir member, to examine whether he or she wants to be identified with any new developments.

Above all, pray and try to understand what God is saying to you about your worship and about some of the underlying causes of apathy or weariness. Life moves in phases like the seasons. Sometimes we are in a season of new growth and things are very exciting. Other times we are experiencing a withdrawal or retraction of the work. As in autumn, areas are dying off and the ministry is gradually becoming bare and fruitless. This need not be seen as negative. In these times God may be stripping our ministry to establish new priorities. We may need a time of fallowness in order to regain our strength and energy for a new period of growth. It is good to build into the life of a ministry regular times of reassessment to give the opportunity for change or to encourage new gifts or new leadership to surface. People often become depressed, weary or frustrated when roles are set and there appears to be no escape from an unending task. It is therefore good to set limits on what is expected of people and even to set a time scale of commitment, so that a person can opt out at the end of the time if circumstances change.

10) Relationship Problems

If the devil can cause suspicion or division between people, he has grasped one of the most effective weapons for destroying the work of the Kingdom. Music is so crucial in the area of worship that it is one of the ministries most vulnerable to this kind of attack. We might usefully identify two main problem areas: *Between Groups* and *Within Groups*.

More and more these days we are seeing the development of small guitar groups springing up to cater for a new style of music which the robed choir is not used to. The church wants to move forward but does not want to cause offence and trauma by sacking the traditional body of very loyal people. Usually the two come to exist side by side in an uneasy compromise. Suspicion and bad feeling begin to grow between the different parties and the situation begins to sour the whole life of the church.

The existence of two separate leadership groups in music is not ideal and says little for the vision of unity in worship. We don't want to throw the traditional element out of the window, but we desperately need to move forward. The vicar, as usual, is caught on the horns of a dilemma and doesn't want to offend anybody. Sometimes he will back-track furiously if he catches the scent of confrontation! However, things will inevitably surface again later on.

What is happening under the surface in these problems? Usually antagonism, obstinacy or anger spring from fear and insecurity. The traditional choir see the new music as a threat to their existence; they don't understand the new concept of worship – it has so far been outside their Christian experience. They may even be jealous that they no longer hold the limelight.

The singing group feels insecure in its new role – often the members have more of a feel for worship than they do for music and are constantly looking over their shoulders to see what the 'professionals' are making of it. They react strongly when attacked on their style of approach and are very jealous of their new-found freedom, refusing to be identified with the choir in its emphasis on musical technique or in wearing robes. Like many renewal groups they are struggling for existence and are making a lot of noise in the process!

Understanding our reactions helps us to begin to overcome them. Most likely, the newer group will need to make the first move towards reconciliation. They are the 'usurpers' and, after all, the choir has been around a very long time before they came on the scene. The singing group may also be more able to pray and share together about the difficulties and discuss what to do.

If fear and insecurity come from ignorance, then the best approach is to begin to communicate. Make friends with those who do not understand you. Listen to their point of view, try and identify with their situation. Win them over by your friendship and concern and establish trust and confidence in you as people. This may mean joining the choir and being prepared to be led by the organist in a different style of music. Sing their style of music, even if you would prefer something with a good beat!

If you are a traditionalist, be tolerant and try to make compromises to the new approach. Don't dismiss something that you are not used to as rubbish. Even if it is, others are obviously deriving much pleasure and meaning from it! Looking down your nose at them is not going to win them over to your point of view. You might even end up actually enjoying the rhythmic vitality or expressive quality of this new music.

If there are tensions between groups or individuals, remember to listen first to their opinion before you have any right to impose your own. You will not be able to influence them otherwise: 'Convince a man against his will, he's of the same opinion still!'

The other common area of relationship problems is *within groups*. If you want to get to know someone, try working with them. In church, we get on fine reading the Bible, praying and even discussing issues; but try a practical team project and we soon see who are the dominant characters, who won't co-operate and who gets trodden on and ordered about.

A music group is a similar place of discovery: the older contralto has a name for being very spiritual and begins to dominate the prayer time or discussion about worship; the instrumentalist won't co-operate by playing what you want – he has a much better way of strumming or improvising; another 'prima donna' sings too loudly or out of tune and is spoiling the whole group's perform-ance; it really is time for an elderly member of the choir to retire – she has a four-inch vibrato and can't keep up with the demands, but she hangs on. How can the poor music leader cope? He didn't really want to lead it in the first place but the vicar insisted and there wasn't anyone else!

I have mentioned the need to be open and honest with one another and of speaking the truth in love. As the leader you have the responsibility and duty to exercise your authority for the greater good. Begin by taking the person aside and gently expressing your concern or objection to what they are doing. Don't get at them in public with sarcastic, sidelong remarks or horizontal prayers. If the member is genuinely committed they will

usually be mortified that they are offending others and
stop doing it. Sometimes they will react strongly, leave
the group or blame you. If you are honestly sure that
what you are saying is right, don't compromise or surrender to feelings of guilt. The other person must come to
terms with his reaction and making things easier by
back-tracking will not help them in the long run.

Perhaps the situation is more serious. In one singing
group a difficult lady was subject to moods and temper
tantrums. She spent most of the practice time splayed out
on the floor making it impossible for the group to carry on
its task. This kind of problem requires some more expert
help. Some things are too big for the group to handle. It is
always good to be covered by an outside 'elder' of some
kind. This might be the minister, who can bring pastoral
guidance or authority and, if the relationship is beyond
reasonable argument, can act as a mediator to open up
the difficulty and get both parties to be objective. I
have mentioned how useful shared leadership can be in
de-personalising policies and decisions in a group.

Try to be ruthless in maintaining your openness and
honesty. 'Maintain the unity of the Spirit in the bond of
peace,' as the Bible says, but do it in love. Don't look for
confrontation if the issue isn't that important. Constantly
think of the health and well-being of the whole group and
don't allow anything to hinder the spirit of worship and
love that you have. A machine needs constant mainte-
nance: oiling bearings, keeping it clean, supplying it with
fuel, and dealing with any problems when they first
occur. Keep your group running efficiently by correcting
faults early!

11) Lack of Commitment

Another area related to people's attitudes and relationships is the area of commitment. The choir or music

group can't get people to commit themselves to a regular practice time. There is a lack of discipline – people turn up late or not at all and don't let the leader know. They lack concentration in rehearsals and are casual and slip-shod in performance. Sometimes the group has no re-hearsal at all, just a five minute dash through the material before the service. Everyone is so busy and recruitment is a constant headache.

This is a very sorry state of affairs and usually implies a lack of firm leadership. We are so frightened of offending people that we don't dare say anything for fear of upset-ting them. We should take a leaf out of the book of some successful secular choirs! There is one in York which demands total allegiance. A person is required to attend every rehearsal and there are numerous concerts each year. Missing more than three practices means the sack. Each must go through a tough audition to start with and take singing lessons if necessary.

If we expect nothing, we will get back exactly what we expect! Surely the ministry of leading worship is worthy of all-out commitment? Sort out the wheat from the tares by setting out the aims of your group and exactly what you require of people. Give them a vision of the ministry which the group has by teaching them, either by your-self, or with the minister. Thrill people with the potential of music in worship and show how worthwhile it is. Don't worry if some feel they can't be involved. Spread the message far and wide and concentrate on getting people with a sense of calling, a desire to commit them-selves and the loyalty and perseverance to see it through. Don't go for great numbers or musical brilliance instead!

Finally, remember to be committed yourself. You won't get very far as a leader if you keep missing practices, start late or prepare badly.

12) P.A.

P.A. means Public Address and refers to a system of sound reinforcement. The musical purist is horrified by the thought of any electronic violation of the music, but sometimes P.A. is necessary. I have seen a guitar concerto performed in a famous concert hall where the balance between soloist and orchestra was so unequal that P.A. had to be used. In church a similar situation may exist between guitars and organ for example. In our own church the congregation is so overwhelming in numbers and volume when they sing, that the only way the choir and instrumentalists can give an adequate lead and accompany effectively is through the use of P.A.

The P.A. is like another musical instrument and it is vital to understand this. It needs to be of high quality especially if it is to be used for music. A speech system will be hopeless for music. Furthermore, if the P.A. is good, it may then show up the poor quality of musical instruments. If we have cheap guitars, dead strings or haven't tuned correctly, all these will be magnified by the P.A. The P.A. operator must also be skilled on his instrument. Nothing is more frustrating than preparing music with good tone and balance only to have it destroyed by the man twiddling the knobs! Ideally he should be a musician too.

The other important use of P.A. is in leading worship, where this involves larger numbers. P.A. can provide an intimacy and ease of communication which cannot be accomplished acoustically. It becomes destructive in a smaller group however, where its unnecessary use makes it a barrier to communication; sometimes blasting people out of their seats or making leaders look rather pretentious. If you are thinking of installing or revamping a P.A. system, do get expert advice and make sure you consult the musicians!

13) Copyright

Whenever a church is introducing new music for worship
or creating a new or expanded song-book, it is bound to
run into the question of copyright. In this country, any
original material is automatically the copyright of the
author or composer, whether registered or not; *proving* it
is the difficulty!

There have been problems enough in the secular world
over this issue recently, but in Christian circles there are
further complications. Should a Christian artist, who has
a God-given gift, make claim to own it and then charge a
fee for its use? Surely the Holy Spirit is the source of
inspiration and therefore the material automatically belongs to all of God's people? If we think this way, we see
no problem about copying and using other people's
songs without asking permission. For others, there is a
nagging feeling that what they are doing is not quite
right, but then, who is going to know? When we are faced
with a four-line chorus consisting mostly of 'Hallelujahs'
and three common chords, what right has it to be copyright in the first place?!

The case for copyright can be argued in this way.
Firstly, many Christian musicians rely on sales of records, song-books and royalty fees for their existence.
The Community of Celebration, which produce the
Fisherfolk music, would not survive without them. If we
illegally copy their records and music we are, in effect,
depriving them of their livelihood and stealing what is
their rightful due as labourers in God's kingdom.

Secondly, if we value worship and the ministry of
music, shouldn't we be prepared to invest money in it?
Churches regularly come up with thousands of pounds
for the renovation of buildings and organs – what about
£200 for the material to make our worship live? On a
very practical level, the more we copy music, the less

publishers are able or willing to invest money in providing us with new material. We therefore cut our own throats.

Whatever the moral aspects of the debate, the copyright issue is being taken more and more seriously. You will have to decide whether small amounts of reproduction are worth troubling over, or whether one-off, emergency usage breaks the spirit of the law. However, people are being taken to court by publishers and this may soon be the case in Christian circles. I heard, for instance, of one big American company who sued a convent in Australia for thousands of dollars for infringing copyright. It obviously becomes more black and white when a secular publisher takes over Christian material and has no moral qualms about enforcing its copyright policy.

In our own small publishing business, Mustard Seed Recordings, we had an amusing incident. One person proudly sent us an exact photocopied version of one of our songbooks, even to the extent of copying the covers on similar coloured card. We weren't quite sure what he was trying to prove, but his version must have cost more than the original, unless of course, he had done it at work!

There is obviously one perfect solution: write your own material!

8

INTO THE FUTURE

1) Change is Inevitable

There is only one thing we can be certain of as we stand
looking into the future – things are going to change.
Change is an unavoidable part of life. The seasons
change inexorably from one to another, our bodies change
as they grow older, relationships change as people make
new friends and lose touch with old ones. Change is
particularly noticeable in today's world where the pace of
life is many times faster and more disturbing than for the
previous generation. Our environment is changing –
new houses and factories are being built on what was
once open country. A small copse where I used to play as
a little boy is now a fire-station. Values and moral attitudes, once taken for granted by previous generations,
are now questioned or overturned. What is there in life
that we can use as an anchor to hold us steady? Even the
Church, once a bastion of authority, guidance and comfort, appears to be in a state of confusion. Clergy and
theologians are seen questioning the very fundamentals
of faith. Traditional forms of worship are under siege
from the new and unfamiliar. In the cathedral close, it
may still be possible to pretend that 'God's in his heaven,
all's right with the world' but at local level the Church
is only too aware of the apathy and indifference of ordinary people towards its message.

The prospect of change can fill us with fear. As we look at the position of the Church at the end of the twentieth century we could be very worried indeed! All around us we see diminishing congregations, redundant churches, a lack of money, manpower and resources. Meanwhile the world rushes on into population explosion, genetic engineering, even self-annihilation. We are tempted to close the church door and hide away in the cosy comfort of familiar words, music and traditions, placing our security in the next life because this one holds no hope for us. It has been a brutal shock for many to realise that the Church's relationship with society is no longer what it used to be – we have almost been left on the shelf.

2) Change can be Positive

Coming to terms with change is one of the highest priorities the Church faces today. This has been made much more difficult because we have avoided the challenge for so long. Instead of steadily renewing and adapting our structures and traditions year by year down the centuries, we have largely left things to run their own course. Unfortunately, things never remain static. If they are not growing and evolving, they are stagnating and dying instead. Today we are faced with some parts of the Church which appear to be in the advanced stages of decay. All life seems to have gone out of them; even if the breath of the Spirit visited them, it seems impossible that they could change or respond.

But with God all things are possible. In fact, only when we realise our extreme need and our complete weakness without him can he begin to act. This was certainly the case when David and Anne Watson first came to St. Cuthbert's in 1965. The church had a congregation of about half a dozen and was threatened with redundancy.

What could be done? Humanly the situation was desperate, but the Watsons believed they had a vision for the church and began to pray and fast for its renewal. Bit by bit, with clear Biblical preaching, the creation of a family service and a church fellowship, numbers began to grow.

We can therefore face change in two ways – lament it, indulge in self-pity, fear it and bury our heads in the sand; or regard it positively as a challenge and an opportunity for something new to happen. It is exciting to realise that God is at work in many areas of the Church worldwide. Old patterns of life and worship may be changing, but there is a new honesty and openness to examine where we've gone wrong and what we can do about it.

Our security must be in God. If we are tempted to trust in people, money or traditions, we can be sure that at some point they will be taken away. Nothing must usurp God's position in our lives and in the life of his Church. If we do not respond, he will find other ways, other people to accomplish his will in the world.

This is just as true for church music. We face a tremendous challenge at this point in history. All the trusted heritage of music which has been perfected and developed over centuries appears under threat from a new and alien worship, worlds away from what we have known and come to love. How are we to respond? With a siege mentality, strengthening the battlements and retreating behind them? Or by making an attempt to understand the new developments and the reasons why they have come about?

If we wish, as musicians, to preserve the best of our traditions it is vital that we establish a dialogue with those involved. The vicar who throws out the robed choir and introduces guitars and 'spiritual nursery rhymes' can be forgiven if all he has received from us is obstinacy and intransigence.

This is a very important moment. We are faced with tremendous opportunities to influence what is happening to our church music. It is my fear that we will hang back for the sake of holding on to our positions and opinions and that the mass of church music will slip into the hands of those who have little taste or training, but who do know how to cater for popular demand. We will then have lost the right to influence and shape the music of worship in the vast majority of places.

The time has come to look for a new breed of church musician, not perhaps the ones with brilliant virtuoso gifts of performance, but the ones who are able to get the best from others and who understand their ministry and are willing to serve with their gifts. The Church needs sensitive and creative men and women able to evolve a homogeneous expression of worship which embraces old and new, and where nothing exists, however artistically worthy or beautiful, which does not express the life of the Spirit at work today.

Most of these will be part-time in their duties, but some surely need to be full-time. Maybe there should be some official funding from the denominations for the nurturing of music at a local level? Perhaps musical resource centres could be set up, in the different dioceses of the Anglican Church for example, where local people could come for help and encouragement and where professional church musicians could give advice and go out to individual churches to train and guide them?

Perhaps the cathedrals could help in this respect? They have the facilities and they certainly have the musicians. I wonder if our many cathedral organists are up to the challenge of sharing their wide skill and experience on a local level, where such gifts are so badly needed? Not to reproduce mini cathedral choirs everywhere, but to help form a style of worship which maintains musical quality but which really serves the locality. I know of one place where this is happening and where the organist goes round to different churches holding workshops and seminars on music in worship. The need is desperate, but what a profound effect this could have on the worship and witness of the Church in this land!

There are many signs today that God is shaking up the Church to make it ready and prepared for the future. There is an openness to the Gospel among people that was not there even a decade ago. We seem to have reached the bottom of the decline which the Church has been experiencing for many years now. Some churches may indeed be dying, but there are obvious signs of growth and renewal in many others. We are being forced to adapt to new situations. Music has a very vital role in all this, and the church musician must decide how he needs to adapt and change his ministry. And change he must, if he is not to be left as the curator of various museum pieces in a spiritual backwater. The opportunities are enormous, but are we prepared to meet them, or will we find ourselves sidestepped and left behind?

APPENDIX

BIBLIOGRAPHY

Renewal in Worship – Michael Marshall Marshall, Morgan & Scott 1982

Sing God a Simple Song – Betty Pulkingham Marshall Pickering 1986

Sounds of Wonder – Eddie Ensley Paulist Press 1977

The Worship of God – Ralph Martin Eerdmans 1982

Church Music in a Changing World – Lionel Dakers Mowbray's 1984

Using the Bible in Music – Andrew Maries Bible Society 1983

You are My God – David Watson Hodder & Stoughton 1983

I Believe in the Church – David Watson Hodder & Stoughton 1978

DISCOGRAPHY

Mustard Seed Recordings: c/o St. Cuthbert's Centre, Peasholme Green, York, YO1 2PW, UK

'With Thanksgiving' – Record, Cassette and Song-book

'Peace with the Father' – Record, Cassette and Song-book

'Come and Worship' – Record, Cassette and Song-book

'Behold the Man' – Record, Cassette and Song-book

Celebration Services:
'Cry Hosanna' – Record and Cassette distributed Kingsway Music
'Cry Hosanna' Song-book publ. Hodder & Stoughton 1980
'Lo He Comes' – Record and Cassette distrib. Kingsway

SOURCES OF HELP

Music in Worship Weekend Conferences in Yorkshire with Andrew Maries Contact: The Warden, Lamplugh House, Thwing, Nr. Driffield, E. Yorks, YO25 0DY
Royal School of Church Music Courses on Church Music Contact: The Warden, Addington Palace, Croydon, Surrey, CR9 5AD
Music in Worship Trust – New Resources for Worship Contact: The Secretary, Music in Worship Trust, 151 Bath Rd., Hounslow, Mddx, TW3 3BT

SAMPLE SERVICES

WHIT SUNDAY Family Service 26 May 1985 10.30 a.m.

Title: The Spirit Comes (Organised Heworth, Hull Rd., Groups)
Leader: Graham Cray   Preacher: Chris Cullwick
Organist: Peter Seymour Banners: Pentecost Set Stage & Screen needed
Prepare Congregation: Colin Briant

Sing Praises 44 'Sweet Jesus' + Dance
Confession/Absolution
Choruses: SP115 'In the presence' (Cry Hosanna SB 20)
Laura Hunt age 3

'Flag flying high' (action song) Solomon Nugondi

S. of L.W. 106 'Butterfly Song' (action song) Kate Abboton

Creed

SP 52 'When the Poor and Needy Seek Water' (With Thanksgiving p. 2)

Prayers: Smart Family

Reading + Mime: Acts 2: 1–8, 38, 39

Hymn 245 'Gracious Spirit Dwell With Me' + OFFERING Talk

Worship: SP 92 'He is Here' (Come Together SB)

SP 33 'The Rain Song' (Cry Hosanna SB 106)

S. of L.W. 59 'Fear Not, Rejoice and Be Glad'

Dance on the forecourt after:

'Israeli Water Dance'

'This Is the Day'

'Happy, Happy Are the People'

'On Tiptoe' (Fresh Sounds 84)

EVENING SERVICE 30 June 1985 6.30 p.m.

Title: Do Not Quench The Spirit

Leader: Jane Morris Preacher: Chris Cullwick

Organist: Andrew Maries Worship Leaders: Russell Hodgson, Jeni Farnhill

Guitarists: Chris and Gale P.A.: Paul Harper, Ian Kilden

Banners: Pentecost Set Prepare Congregation: Walter Stockdale

Hymn: 216 'Rejoice the Lord is King'

Confession/Absolution

Praise: SP94 'I Will Enter his Gates'

SP82 Ps. 100 'O be joyful' (Cry Hosanna 120)

Fresh Sounds 105 'Come to the Waters'

Etc . . .

Tear Fund Rep.: John Jackson
Hymn 480 'May the Mind of Christ my Saviour' +
  OFFERING
Reading
SP 89 'And You Shall Know the Truth' (Come and
  Worship SB 4)
Sermon
CHOIR: 'Seeing You Daily' (original anthem)
Prayers: Sue Collier
Worship: S. of L.W. 25, 8 fold Alleluia
           'Jesus, We Enthrone You'
           'Majesty'
           SP125 'The King Is Among Us' (Come and
           Worship SB15)
           Etc . . .
(Prayer and further ministry took place after the service)

ST. MICHAEL-LE-BELFREY CHOIR

Aims and Duties:
'Spiritual'

1. To encourage the spirit of worship among the whole
    congregation, seeking to build them up through our
    praise.
2. To know a sense of calling to the ministry of leading
    in worship and to seek to strengthen and develop
    that ministry in every way, taking it seriously and
    conscientiously.
3. To lead, not only musically, but also by example of life
    and conduct.
4. To work together to create a place of love and accept-
    ance, where we can grow and mature as people, and
    express through our lives corporately what we sing.
5. To give ourselves to one another and the group,
    particularly in prayer and sharing, that we may build

up one another in love at every opportunity.

6. To pray for the worship of St. Michael's and for its leadership, especially Andrew as Musical Director, and Graham as Vicar, seeking to love and support them as over us in the Lord; avoiding gossip and party spirit.

7. To seek daily to be filled with the Spirit and to grow spiritually.

'Practical'

1. To attend all Sunday Evening Services and Wednesday evening rehearsals with the exception of a few a year. Also, to be open to the possibility of helping at Family Services and other special services (e.g. Good Friday, Lunch Hours etc.) unless circumstances do not permit.

2. To submit requests for absence to the Director in good time – at least a fortnight, except in special circumstances, bearing in mind a responsibility to provide a balanced ensemble for Sunday worship.

3. To be punctual and reliable members, ready to start rehearsing at the time stated: Wednesday – 7.00 p.m.; Sunday Evening – 5.45 p.m.; Family Service – 9.30 a.m.

4. To concentrate and be attentive during rehearsals, and to be responsible in preparing, ordering and bringing music for the various meetings.

5. To aim at improving musical abilities in every way possible, that we may be well equipped, never letting ourselves become complacent in these things.

NOTE: Choir members are expected to have been committed to the church, preferably in an Area Group for at least six months before joining, and to have their support and encouragement. (This does not apply to students.)

A TYPICAL CHOIR PRACTICE

7.00   *Hymn* (or sometimes physical exercises to relax and settle people).

7.05   *General Notices* relating to forthcoming services, events and arrangements. *Sharing of general prayer needs or news.*

7.20   *Either*:   a *Worship Time* with praise, worship, sharing, teaching and prayer.

       Or: *Cell Groups* of 6–8 for mutual support and more personal prayer and sharing.

       These operate alternate weeks.

8.00 (8.15)   Sometimes some simple *Vocal Exercises*.

8.10   Learning *New Pieces* (perhaps a traditional anthem or a new arrangement) or working on items of greater difficulty for a fortnight ahead. Sometimes *Sectional Rehearsals* in which men and women split up to do 'note bashing' on new pieces. This economises on time.

8.30   *Break* for Orange Squash (10p is charged for this to finance the Choir Fund which pays for leaving presents, baby gifts etc.). Time to relax and chat.

8.40   *Music for Sunday* (the Choir mainly exists for the evening services, volunteers help in the informal Family Service Group).
Running through introductions, rehearsing with other instruments – piano, guitar, bass, oboe, clarinet etc. (Instrumentalists usually come from within the choir – this creates greater unity. We cannot practice with the organ as we meet in another building). Generally touching up our repertoire.

9.30   Finish promptly with prayer or the Grace. (Once a month we finish earlier at 9.00 to have an open business meeting to discuss the life and running of the choir.)